SPIRAL

A Catalyst for Innovation and Expansion

AMY SIMPKINS

Positively Powered Publications

Positively Powered Publications
PO Box 270098
Louisville, CO 80027
PositivelyPoweredAuthors.com

Cover Design: Melody Christian of FinickyDesigns.com
Project Editor: Amy Collette
Proofreading Editor: Lauren Brombert

Ordering Information: PositivelyPoweredAuthors.com

Quantity sales: Special discounts are available on quantity purchases by nonprofit organizations, corporations, associations, clubs and others. For details, contact us at PositivelyPoweredAuthors.com

SPIRAL / Amy Simpkins —1st ed.

ISBN: 978-0-9961692-7-1

Praise for *Spiral*

"Amy knows her stuff, because she has done it, after doing well in the very demanding environment at MIT and then the space program. She is one of only a few serial tech entrepreneurs who have the ability to synthesize their sustained and varied experiences—left brain and right brain—and present the learnings in ways that others can benefit from as they think about building their own new business. Entrepreneurship and starting new businesses is not for everyone. Reading Amy's book will help you to decide if you are ready to take the grueling journey."

~Ken Morse, Serial Entrepreneur, Tech Angel Investor, Founding Managing Director, MIT Entrepreneurship Center

"Amy Simpkins is the Patti Smith of innovation. Like a punk rocker, it's all about the creation and not about the labels people routinely accept. *Spiral* is truly new thinking about innovation. I'm intrigued by the approach and will be integrating it into my own tool chest. This is a fresh, direct, personal, insightful, empowering, de-mythologizing, and well-written book about innovation. It's new, different, and useful; in other words, innovative. I highly recommend it."

~Gregg Fraley, Author, CEO, and Innovation Consultant

"I wish I had had *Spiral* as my guidebook to light the way on my own creative journey. This book is a treasure trove abound with perspective shifts, tools, and frameworks that will help you realize that the creative journey matters more than the destination, and that you need not expect to travel that journey is a straight line. In fact, all the best learning, goodness, and revelation happens in the spiral. This is a book you will need your highlighter for, you will want to read it again and again. You'll be sharing the lessons of *Spiral* with your children."

~Julie Neale, Founder, Coach and Community
Builder at Mother's Quest

"Amy Simpkins offers us an engaging, personal guide—a kind of companion—in our struggles through the universal phases of development. It may be personal development, or business or product development. She says 'I believe in you,' and by the end of her book we feel she means it.

Spiral uses a conversational, personal style, reading easily and quickly but inviting re-reading, which is consistent with her use of the spiral. It is full of practical questions posed to us, drawn from her own experience—a personal journey of a scientist discovering a better creative process, broadly applicable.

I have probably written a hundred business plans, profit and nonprofit. None of them ever happened as planned, but in many cases something did. *Spiral* describes why."

~David S. Dayton, Chairman,
Clean Energy Solutions, Inc.

"In *Spiral*, Amy Simpkins passionately shares her insight into the wisdom of cycles. She helps us understand the naturally occurring ebb and flow, whether in our personal or business development, so we not only embrace but engage with these cycles. *Spiral* teaches us to use the slower, less productive times to recharge so that we move forward during the creative periods and faster in times of growth. This could not have been a timelier read for me during my intentional break from the corporate world."

~Tamara DaSantos, former Finance Manager, Bell Helicopter

"Amy Simpkins shows you how to write your own love letter; think about the impossible! Rethink how you see yourself. Learn how to stop the little voice in your head talking you out of your dreams. *Spiral* will guide you to weave your own path to success. Outstanding read!"

~Christine Daspro, Founder and CEO, Curating Connections

"This book is for anyone who has a dream, life, or vision they fear might be too big or radical. Let Amy help broaden your horizons and dream, live, envision even more with this inspiring and practical book. I appreciate Amy's holistic approach: building on all of our strengths and perceived weaknesses. As a new entrepreneur myself, I have gained many helpful insights for moving forward with my writing and my business. I resonate very strongly with many of her ideas and revolutionary observations."

~Crystal Dyste, Author and Indie Publisher,
Dyste Writing and Publishing

"I clearly saw what has impeded me in the past—fighting the rhythms, trapped in "this or that" thinking. This new wisdom is now spiraling in my head to support me in utilizing the gifts and wisdom available to me in each present moment and embracing wherever I am. I devoured every word! Amy Simpkins is one badass woman!"

~Shauna Karine, Soul Doula

"*Spiral* provides a much-needed framework for sustainable growth, in business and life. Amy Simpkins brilliantly describes how the natural growth cycles support creative processes, business growth as well as personal growth. In this book, she combines science, structure, and engineering with creativity, intuitive wisdom, and spirituality, paving the way for visionary business owners and entrepreneurs of the new purpose-driven economy. A must read!"

~Willemijn Maas, MD, Founder of Elemental Life

"Through a diversity of experiences, Amy Simpkins (an MIT-trained rocket scientist turned serial entrepreneur) brings together a fusion of engineering methodology, business best principles, and emotional connection to create a practical, actionable framework for burgeoning entrepreneurs to grow their businesses."

~Ben Ruedlinger, Chief of Business Operations at Wistia

"*Spiral* is a book you would do well to cycle through more than once. This fascinating book walks the reader through the iterative process that engineers and tech companies are already using to develop technology, but frames them within a much broader, life-enhancing model. The reader is guided past the technical iterative mechanics of the factory processes and out into the colorful rainforest of creative possibilities."

~Shannon Scarlett, Principal and Owner,
Shannon Scarlett Architects

Bonus Material

YOU ARE THE HERO OF YOUR OWN CREATOR'S JOURNEY.

You have received the call to create something amazing in your work or in your life. Though you are eager to see your vision become reality, you may be facing all the fears and perceived roadblocks and "what ifs" that come with accepting such a call. By holding this book in your hand, you are meeting a mentor for this journey and holding a framework that can guide you on the road ahead. As you cross the threshold toward doing this sacred work in the world, there will be challenges, tests, and ordeals. There will be allies, victories, and rewards. You're going to need tools in your toolbox to help you along the way. This book is your first tool.

FOR MORE TOOLS TO HELP YOU HARNESS THE POWER OF YOUR OWN SPIRAL, head over to

http://amysimpkins.com/spiralbonus.

You'll get instant access to exclusive bonus content, including the **Spiral Journey Tracker**, a simple visual tool to help you keep track of where you are in your own personal spirals and how to leverage them.

Dedication

To Andrew, the maker. May you manifest creations of utility, strength, and beauty.

To Clara, the lioness. May you embrace your softness and ferocity, and use them both in their turn.

To Nathaniel, the sage. May the edges of your wisdom and your compassion lead the way.

Table of Contents

Foreword

AS AN ELECTRICAL ENGINEER BY EDUCATION, it took me a long time to accept that my real appreciation is for creativity, writing, storytelling, poetry, art, drawing and spirituality. I see engineers and scientists in one corner and artists in another. I've never met someone who was able to not only identify with both engineering and art in equal measures, but go even one step further and show that engineering is art. Science is art. And in the case of this book, even business development is art through the lens of spiral design. Ladies and gentlemen, I give you Amy Simpkins and *Spiral: A Catalyst for Innovation and Expansion.* Amy's unique take on business will leave you spellbound.

Right out of the gate, Amy asks us to reconsider the labels we give ourselves, for beware the limitations they impose on our identity. We are all problem solvers, innovators, engineers, creators and creatives, artists and architects. She helps us embrace the fact that what we want through the course of our lives can and will change and that is by grand design.

As a coach, I work with business owners, entrepreneurs, and individuals with big dreams. Every one of them is looking for the shortest path to traverse point A (their current state) to point B (their ultimate dream state). Everyone wants the straight line there. They have some expectations of setbacks and plateaus, failures and successes, but otherwise, "Give me the roadmap in the most efficient and clean way possible, pretty please."

In this beautiful book, we learn that the linear process is not always the answer, and that linear thinking can often lead us astray and leave us disappointed. Amy Simpkins takes us gently through all the natural cycles, the stuff that makes up dreams and visions. We learn to be flexible and embrace the beautiful spirals that these cycles create to move us from one moment into the next and to pave the road to innovation. As Amy says, "We are not robots. We are messy, organic, evolutionary beings who are always growing, always learning, always changing."

Once you get this, you can be more comfortable with all that shows up as you fiercely pursue your dreams because—make no mistake—Amy is not here to tell you to tone down those dreams or to think any smaller. Quite the opposite! She prepares you for thinking and dreaming bigger than you ever have and encourages you to find a path that doesn't kill you along the way.

While the message may be as simple as accepting where we are in the exact point in our journeys, the articulation of this message is one of a kind as Amy takes us through the deep yet crystal clear understanding of how we as humans naturally fluctuate between right and left, between focus and distraction, between rest and unrest, between work and play, between feminine and masculine. That is exactly how we are meant to operate. So why fight it? Amy argues that every time we fight the natural spiral, we lose. Instead, if we go with the flow, we can even reach a state of effortless joy. In the thick of the book, Amy takes us through the spiral phases and gives us powerful insights about the practical application of each phase.

I have had the pleasure of working with Amy and watching her on her own spiral journey. I have never doubted her brilliance, and this book is a delightful surprise as Amy brings her unique perspective of business and personal development to light. There are so many powerful insights in this book. I will leave you with one more below and let you discover the rest on your own as you turn the pages.

We are not as divided as we're prone to think. We can be feminine and masculine, introvert and extrovert, focused and distracted, depending on the cycle in which we find ourselves. She breaks down this mental construct and gives us a new lens, a fresh perspective. She teaches us the importance of having both structure and flow in the work of achieving our life purpose. She asks us to see and accept the cycles in order to achieve our greatest potential. "What if we embraced the need for iteration? What if we embraced that an individual human on a week-to-week basis or month-to-month basis may have different skills coming to the forefront, may have different preferences, may be able to perform at different levels on different tasks? What if we embraced that?"

Can you do that? I will most certainly be giving it my best shot!

Farnoosh Brock, Business and Leadership Coach
Founder of Prolific Living Inc.
Author of *The Serving Mindset: Stop Selling and Grow Your Business*

PART I: THE BEGINNING

CHAPTER ONE

All the Things You Are
(A Love Letter)

HUMANS ARE FUNNY ABOUT LABELS. Labels make us feel more secure and validated about who it is we are inside. It's like looking at a rainbow. There are infinite colors in a rainbow. But somehow, we're taught in school that there are seven colors. ROY G BIV, remember? Red, orange, yellow, green, blue, indigo, violet. It makes it easier to label or categorize or limit colors. Why seven, I wonder? And who decided that indigo made the list anyway?

We humans are the same about ourselves. Inside we contain infinite possibilities of things we could be, do, accomplish, or contribute to. But we like the labels. We label all of the different hats we wear and then justify what we do or don't do based on those hats. And those hat labels.

So, before we dive in deep, I want to start by getting you used to the idea that you are all of the following things:

You are a problem solver.

You are an innovator.

You are an engineer.

You are a creator.

You are creative.

You are an artist.

You are an architect.

You may read some of these statements and want to scream, "No! I'm not that!" And I'm curious as to why that is. Is it because you don't want the responsibility of that label? Is it because you don't think you have the skills, education, or experience for it? Is it because you're afraid of being judged against a rubric that corresponds to that label, and you're afraid you won't measure up?

Whatever the reason, I'm here to challenge your self-perception and to help you embrace these facets of your diamond personality that, for whatever reason, are tough for you to accept.

This is important because as we dive deeper we're going to talk about some big ideas and revolutionary concepts. I'm going to ask you to take on these labels, to wear these hats, and to think differently than you might be used to. I have no doubt that you have the capability to do this. Regardless of your education (labels), job title (labels), Myers-Briggs Type Indicator (MBTI—also labels), or claimed Harry Potter Hogwarts house (yep, labels again), you have a rainbow of potential inside you with an infinite spectrum of possibility.

You have all this in you—and more.

You Are a Problem Solver

Let's start with an easy one. Your lizard brain probably won't start squawking if I give you the problem-solver hat, am I right? You're used to finding solutions on the daily to all the mundane stuff that happens in your life. Taking that a step farther, as a business owner, you're a problem solver for your clients. No matter what field you are in or what you are offering, you're being asked regularly to solve the problems of your clients. And you have solutions to do just that.

You Are an Innovator

If you come to terms with your problem-solver hat, it's not a terribly giant leap of logic to say that you are an innovator. You innovate when you're presented with a problem (yours or a client's), and you come up with a solution for it. Sometimes you simply deliver a well-known solution that has been delivered before.

"That doesn't seem all that innovative," I hear you protest. But any time you customize, tailor, present from a different perspective, or combine several well-known things into a new formula, my friend, you innovate. Innovation takes two main forms—incremental innovation and disruptive innovation. Incremental innovation means improving upon something that already exists—doing it better. Disruptive innovation means creating a new solution— doing it differently. You possess the power of innovation as you solve problems and present solutions. You are an innovator.

You Are an Engineer

I love this one and instantly relate to it, having had the word *engineer* in my job title for about 15 years. However, I know this word can sometimes cause inner conflict, especially if your job title doesn't explicitly contain the word. It's okay if that's you, but I want you to ease into that sense of panic that just came up for you and consider for a moment that you may actually be an engineer after all.

An engineer is someone who deliberately designs solutions to a problem, seeks to find out if her solution is the best one (or at least a great one), and then tests it to see if she's right. This process is a natural, human one, and not one to be afraid of or shy away from. You take your inner problem solver, your inner innovator, and you get a little more curious and a little bolder in how you experiment with your ideas. You get a little more rigorous about asking the question "How do I know that my idea, my innovative solution is a good one?" *et voilà* —you've found your inner engineer. She's in there, honey.

You Are a Creator

I know this because you wouldn't be here if you weren't. You're reading this book because you are a creator. I'm asking you this big question here, before we get started on our journey together (because it's important for our journey):

What is it that you are actively creating?

Now the answer could be anything. It could be multiple things. It could be specific, or it could be nebulous. That depends on you. But if I know anything, I know this: you are actively creating something, and I want you to keep that in mind while we walk this journey together.

You could be creating a book.

You could be creating a childhood dream.

You could be creating a fulfilling career.

You could be creating a profitable business that you intend to sell.

You could be creating a lifestyle business that allows you to have the experiences you want.

You could be creating an invention.

You could be creating a life you love.

You could be creating an emotional state of being that you like.

You could be creating a family.

You could be creating a movement.

You could be creating exactly what the world needs.

You could be creating exactly what *you* need.

How do I know this? I have, at one time or another, been creating one or more of these things.

And it's important to establish that you are a creator because there is power in owning that title. There is power in seeing who you are and seeing this role as part of your state of being. There is power in seeing that, no matter where you are, you are on the Creator's Journey.

You're familiar with the Hero's Journey, yes? Joseph Campbell researched a great pile of humanity's literary creations in the early twentieth century. He boiled the common formula for such stories down to the monomyth—the Hero's Journey. It starts with a protagonist going about her mundane, ordinary life, being presented with a task that she seems comically incapable of completing, finding mentors and compatriots (sometimes in unlikely places), fighting the various battles to be fought, and solving the puzzles that need to be solved—before facing the ultimate challenge, completing the task, and heading home, a totally transformed person.

The Creator's Journey is like that.

It's like that with the quest and the mentors and the challenges and the victory. But in the Creator's Journey, the task is changing, the path is changing, and we go on the same journey over and over again, sometimes multiple times, to manifest a single piece of Inspiration.

You Are Creative

This was the hardest one for me to accept in my own journey. I don't know what it is about the word *creative* that's so anathema to me, so triggering. I can follow this line of thinking just fine: I'm a problem solver (definitely), an innovator (sure), an engineer (with the sheepskin to prove it), and a creator (you betcha). But creative? Me?

So, this little love letter is for me as much as it is for you.

You are a creator, therefore you are creative.

It's just that simple.

It's your creativity that allows you to express your true, core self. It's your creativity through which you make anything happen.

The title "creative" isn't reserved for a select and honored few. It's for anyone who is determined to be an active participant in life.

May you and I both realize it, accept it, and harness it.

You Are an Artist

I don't know about you, but somewhere between *creativity* and *artistry*, I have a tendency to get stuck. I used to believe that the title of *artist* was reserved for people who created very specific types of art. Painting and sculpture, for sure, and also dance, music, and theater.

But in reality, isn't art just about the outward expression of creativity? In the same way that everyone has an inner engineer, I believe we all have our inner artist. After all, art is the outward expression of creativity. When we share our inner creations, we are artists.

If you're with me so far, and you are a creator and you are creative, the next logical jump is that you are an artist. If your creativity is wired up to inspiration and self-expression, and you use those tools to put something new into the world, you're an artist.

You Are an Architect

This is where it all comes together.

You are an engineer. You have the power to solve problems—big and small, simple and complex. You're able to think about these solutions in structured and rigorous ways.

You are an artist. You create something where nothing was before. You tap into your own inner mystery of inspiration (though you may not fully understand how that works) to produce solutions that are uniquely *you*.

Architecture is simply the fusion of engineering and artistry.

Since engineering and artistry coexist inside you, you are an architect.

You're probably most familiar with architecture as it applies to buildings. That works. Think of a building architect. The architect of a building is responsible for all the technical pieces of the building design—it has to serve the function it was meant to, whether that's an office space, a residence, or a warehouse. The building design also must meet all the building codes and pass all the inspections. But the best architects, the ones you've heard of and remember, are famous because their buildings are works of art. They possess that *je-ne-sais-quoi* factor that takes your breath away. They are inspiring. They are inspired.

Vitruvius was a Roman architect who wrote one of the first known treatises on architecture, *De architectura*. It's mostly a very thorough description of how to design a bathhouse. But before he gets down to brass tacks, Vitruvius states that in order to be good, architecture must possess three qualities:

- *Utilitas*, or usefulness. The architecture must serve a purpose, solve a problem, or perform a function.

- *Firmitas*, or sustainability. The architecture must be built to last, including standing up to abnormal events such as storms or extreme temperatures.

- *Venustas*, or beauty. R. Buckminster Fuller, one of those famous architects, said, "When I am working to solve a problem, I never think about beauty. I only think about how to solve the problem. But when I have finished, if the solution is not beautiful, I know it is wrong."

You have the capability to bring together usefulness, sustainability, and beauty. You fuse engineering and artistry.

That makes you an architect.

You architect your life.

You architect your work.

You architect the ways you help the world.

This book is a love letter from me to you, to remind you that you are all this and more. To remind you that you have everything you need inside you. All the tools are already in your toolbox.

The thing that's in your heart to bring to the world is possible. And you will be the architect.

CHAPTER TWO

The Backstory

WHEN I WAS 12 YEARS OLD, I decided I would be an astronaut. This wasn't a whim of a career goal as it is for many children. I believed in my heart (and still believe to this day) that if I wanted to do it, worked hard, and put myself in the right places, I would absolutely be able to join the astronaut corps.

Astronaut was a powerful two-sided dream for me. It would be personally fulfilling to fly in space, experience weightlessness, and see the blue marble of Earth with no borders. It would also contribute to humankind by advancing scientific knowledge through the exploration of space. I was passionate about both of these internal and external missions, and every single step I took was calculated to bring me closer to my goal.

I continued this way through high school, through my grueling undergraduate work at MIT, through a master's degree from the University of Southern California, and finally moved to Denver, Colorado, to work on manned spacecraft at Lockheed Martin Space Systems Company. During the first five years of my career, I worked to propose, design, and integrate various types of spacecraft, but I also gained invaluable experience under the tutelage of my first and greatest mentor, Cliff Gates, on unmanned Earth observing satellites, doing performance analysis, architectural assessment, and real-time system simulation.

Throughout this time, I remained 100 percent dedicated to my astronaut aspirations. I told anyone who would listen that I wasn't long for staying here because I would be applying to the astronaut program soon. I told my future husband on our first date that he had better be prepared to move to Houston, Texas, and if he didn't like it, he didn't have to date me.

It was after I'd moved into my dream job—short of being an astronaut, of course—that the strangest thing happened. I'd taken a position with the Cabin and Cockpit Working Group (CWG) on the Orion program, destined to be NASA's next manned spacecraft and the successor to the legacy of the Space Shuttle program. The job was located in Houston, with a desk across the street from Johnson Space Center, where I had free access to observe space station mission control and stroll the hallowed halls of the astronaut office whenever I wanted.

The CWG work was, in hindsight, the most ideally suited work that I ever did as a spacecraft engineer. It was all about integration. We worked the hardest requirements, the ones that demanded cooperation and co-solution from different teams that tended to talk past each other. Solutions to these problems combined analysis, design, collaboration, and operational know-how. My work was one part technical analysis, two parts group facilitation, and one part storytelling about what it would be like to live and work in space aboard Orion.

One of the design challenges I worked on was the net habitable volume of the spacecraft. It was about figuring out how to fit all the necessary equipment into the capsule and still leave space for the astronauts to live in relative comfort. We joked about how we must be the only engineers in the world who worked to build empty space. I had no idea then that I would be writing, coaching, and preaching on the equal importance of structure and empty space in the future. I also worked on hand controls for the computer that would be easy to use in a suit with pressurized gloves, radiation protection protocols for the crew, food-preparation equipment design and operation, and more. Anything that goes along with living and working in space came together under the purview of the CWG and, for a time, me.

I was in my element. I felt powerful. I felt effective. I was completely engaged. I spun narratives that connected with both the design engineers and the crew. I brought teams together that previously couldn't understand what the other was saying. I advocated for holistic solutions to solve hard problems. I was having a blast.

Then it happened. A round of applications for the astronaut program opened up that spring while I was making friends with the crew and coaxing out their deepest needs when it came to eating in space. It was the first time an application round had opened up when I was eligible to apply. As I loaded the job posting page at my desk, a shock of anticipation coursed through me. This was it. This was the moment I'd been waiting for my whole life. Every step I'd taken had led me here, to this moment. I had earned this. Once the application loaded, I scanned the questions, but I didn't begin. This application would take time and consideration, so I would make sure that I was really ready to do it.

The weeks of the application window passed. I would load the page again, stare at the blinking cursor mocking me from the blank boxes, and wait for inspiration to strike about what it was I should write there. It never did.

Eventually, I decided that this hesitation was stupid, and I completed the application with the fallback method through which I had come to accomplish anything hard: brute force. I let the nasty voice in my head tell me I was being ridiculous and scold me for procrastinating, and I banged out the summary of my experience and credentials.

At the end of the page, my mouse cursor hovered over the Submit button. I didn't click it. Recognizing that this was a critical, dramatic moment in the narrative of my life, I savored it. I took a deep breath, heard epic theme music in my mind, and leaned forward. But again, I didn't click the button.

I took my hand off the mouse and slumped back in my desk chair. I ran my fingers through my Texas-big curly hair. I stared at the screen with all my life's work laid out on the page. And the voice that bubbled up from inside me was as clear as a bell.

This isn't what you really want.

I blinked and looked around my cubicle, which sat in an area so isolated that if I didn't get up from my chair for a while, the motion-activated lights would shut off. No one was around.

I got up and paced, casting bewildered glances at my application, my life's work, still beaming out at me from the flat-panel monitor.

What if this isn't what I really want?

What if I don't want this life?

What if I have skills, talents, gifts, and desires that would be more powerfully focused elsewhere?

What if what I really wanted to do was design integration?

What I really want to do is design integration.

What I'm really good at is design integration.

What I'm really called to is design integration.

And then, shockingly...

I don't think I actually want to be an astronaut anymore.

I shut the browser window and locked the screen. *Just for now*, I thought. I walked away from my desk, then out into the oppressive Texas heat, gulping the thick, dense air like it was a cool drink of water. Thoughts of "What do I really want? What if everything I believed to be true has changed?" reverberated in my head.

I called my mentor, Cliff. He told me, "You can do anything you want to do. You have so much inside you. And you get to make the decision about that. But are you sure?"

I called my then-fiancé. "It's not because of me, is it? I would never do anything to hold you back. I fully support whatever you want. But are you sure?"

I was anything but sure.

I didn't know how to be sure of anything anymore, least of all myself.

So, I grabbed at the threads of sense.

This isn't that far off, I mused. Being a design integration engineer who builds manned spacecraft is totally consistent with the original vision: advance human scientific knowledge through the exploration of space. I felt good about it. As I accepted that, it felt good, I felt light. I felt free. There was so much possibility! I saw all of these delicious, hard problems laid out in front of me that needed my special brand of genius to be solved. It was a heady amount of passion drawing me forward, into a new future, and I was beyond excited about it.

I never opened the astronaut application page again.

That was the beginning of listening to my heart calling. That was the first time that I even contemplated the idea that what I wanted could change, would change, was changing.

It turned out that this was a breaking point. From there on out in my career, I started to follow my heart again, which was something hadn't done in a very long time. Being an astronaut, working for the space program, designing spacecraft—all of these things were certainly passions and things that I felt so very connected to. But as I pursued them, somewhere along the way I had stopped paying attention to what my heart was saying, and started to simply follow the prescriptive path laid out in front of me, long and straight.

That moment of turning away from the long-held dream in favor of what I'd learned I was good at, had to offer, and wanted from life— that was me embarking on an adventure, the start of my Creator's Journey.

There's more to the story of my career: how I came to realize that I didn't want to work in the corporate world anymore and how I came to realize that I wanted to be a coach and work with people to build their own visions, to strategize their own dreams; how I grew further still and became CEO of a tech company in the renewable energy sector.

But those stories aren't really the stories of this book. Those stories are just more of the same: choosing to follow my heart, to take opportunities as doors opened in front of me, to feel the tension between having a grand vision and moving toward something big, but also allowing for growth and change in my dreams.

After I left my corporate engineering job and started working as a business strategy coach, I started to see patterns in business development for my clients that greatly resembled the patterns of design that I'd seen in engineering. It occurred to me that a business owner is a person who is designing a business, in the same way that an engineer might design a software system or a spacecraft. Taking this even deeper, we are all the designers of our own life. Creating a life we love is simply an exercise in design. All of the same principles apply across the board, whether you're an engineer, a business owner, or simply a human who really wants to create an amazing, fulfilled life. Good design is good design.

As I dove deeper with clients who were developing businesses, I got really frustrated with messages from leaders in entrepreneurship and marketing about how fast and straightforward it was to build a business. As an entrepreneur myself, I did a lot of reading and listening to podcasts, and I certainly took a lot of courses to tell me how to best put my business together and how to get as many followers, subscribers, and clients as soon as possible. It frustrated me to see message after message telling me that all I needed to do was follow a certain number of very simple steps and I would find success. This linear approach to success or fulfillment seemed disingenuous to me.

I was reminded of the engineering design process. Back in the days of the Apollo program, as we were attempting to send humans to the moon, the engineering community adopted a very straightforward, linear approach to development of technology, sometimes called the Waterfall Method. It was expected that, even when developing an entirely new technical solution, the design process would progress in a straightforward manner from step one to step two to step three and then—boom!—you'd find yourself with a fully developed system, ready to roll.

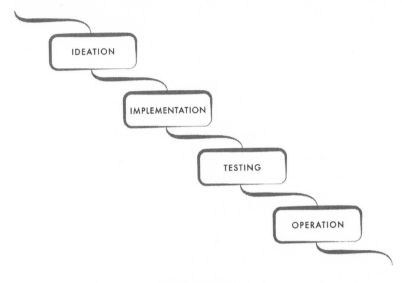

Waterfall Method

Unfortunately, real life rarely progresses so predictably. We're human. We make mistakes. We learn new things. We uncover a new innovation that would make the whole project better. If mistakes were made in the linear design process, project leaders would just throw more resources at it—more manpower, more money—to correct them. Sometimes the mistakes were quite expensive because there was no opportunity given to circle back around and incorporate things that had been learned or course-correct if a new direction was needed.

Once John F. Kennedy said, "We choose to go to the moon," it was expected that we'd just incrementally go through all of the required steps to get there, and—boom!—we'd land on the moon. It turns out that pretty much did happen, but not without a lot of money spent, a huge political movement that drove the development forward, and the loss of a few lives.

Of course, not all technological development has the political force of a Cold War sitting behind it, pushing it forward. So in the years that followed, the linear method of developing new technologies started to fall apart. This was especially true as computers and software matured as an industry and required even more rapid development.

In the mid-1980s, a software engineer by the name of Barry Boehm posited that the linear model of developing a technical system wasn't great. Barry thought that, instead, we should be looking at a spiral methodology for design—one in which design happens iteratively.

Spiral development was born.

CHAPTER THREE

Enter Spiral Development

SPIRAL DEVELOPMENT IS AN ITERATIVE PROCESS that forms the foundation of many different technical design methodologies. This was the first time we said as an engineering community, "Maybe design shouldn't happen from point A to point B in a straight line, just moving through the steps robotically. Maybe there's an evolutionary component to technological development in the same way that there's an evolutionary component to growth."

The steps, or phases, of that design spiral were pretty straightforward. In fact, they were pretty much the same steps of the linear Waterfall method, except that the steps occurred with the fundamental idea that it was normal, expected, and even desirable to go through them several times in sequence, each time around building on the last.

IMPLEMENTATION   IDEATION

TESTING   EVALUATION

Engineering Spiral Development

The first engineering spiral phase is Ideation, where brainstorming happens. The idea is conceived, and you decide what you're going to do. You decide what problem you'll solve and how you'll approach the solution space. You need to decide what the thing you're building will do and how it's going to be different from other solutions. This is an exciting phase for engineering because it's where the innovation really happens.

Once you decide what you're going to do, you move into a phase of Implementation, of actually starting to make that happen—building something that looks like the solution. In early trips around the spiral, Implementation can look like a rapid prototype, a software model, or a simple diagram on the back of a napkin. In later spirals, Implementation starts to look like production hardware that will actually be tested and deployed. Regardless of the level of fidelity, the Implementation phase is where you take the ideas that exist only out in the ether of inspiration and turn them into something real.

The third phase of the development spiral is the Testing phase. Here's where you take your Implementation from the second phase and put it to the test. If it's an idea that's simply sketched on the back of a napkin, the testing may be as simple as a thought experiment. It might be a survey of clients or potential users to gauge what they think about the idea. If it's a prototype, you can do small-scale testing, or if it's a software model, you can do simulated testing. If it's actual production hardware in later phases, then you're going to put it through its paces to make sure that it does what it's supposed to do and meets all of the various requirements that you need it to meet.

And the final phase of the spiral is the Evaluation phase. Once you've done testing on your current version, you take a step back and say, "Okay, what did we learn in this spiral? Are we still on the right track? Is this still the thing we're building? Did we learn anything new that's going to change our direction? Now, how do we go around again?"

When you go around the spiral again, you can take it from a high level to a lower level, from more generalized ideas to more specific and detailed ideas. You go around and around the spiral until you've produced something that you can put out there, either to sell as a product or to do a specific job in the field. That's how you build new technology.

There's a bonus phase of the engineering spiral, in which you get to spin off what you've built and start to sell it while you continue to spiral and develop it further. A great example of how this works is Microsoft's Windows operating system. How many different versions of Windows have there been? Way back, during the initial development of Windows, they didn't wait to deploy it until they knew everything about how a personal computer would be used. They didn't wait to figure out how technology would develop so that the software was infinitely extensible. They built something innovative, and they got it out the door. In the words of Seth Godin, they shipped. And then, while they were selling that first version of Windows, Microsoft was able to develop the next version.

Even to this day, Microsoft is still doing this— releasing a version of Windows while developing the next one. But they don't even wait to ship a version until all the bugs are found. They know it's unlikely that they'll find all the bugs the first time. Instead of waiting for perfection, they trust that they can always issue a security update or a patch.

The same thing is true for lots of different kinds of technologies. Instead of waiting for the be-all-and-end-all version, just start with the first version. Put it out there, ship it, learn what you can, and then ship a better version during the next trip around the spiral.

Consumers are complicit in this arrangement. We don't expect perfection from Microsoft—we expect to be able to use the product to satisfy our immediate needs. We accept that the product is always evolving, and we're a part of that iterative process.

Applying the Spiral

As a business builder, I was seeing the incredibly rigid linear thinking of most business coaches and marketing gurus, and it really turned me off. These were step-by-step processes designed by people I couldn't relate to, comprising steps that happened to work for one person, one time. They claimed that I was going to make six figures within 90 days if I'd just follow these simple steps. When it all came crashing down, I felt like a failure because that flashy success didn't happen. And why? Because I expected a linear process, a simple step-by-step map to solve all my problems, instead of allowing for natural, evolutionary, iterative growth tailored to my own personality, needs, and desires. Once I started coaching other business builders on their own entrepreneurial journeys, I saw this drama play out over and over again, and with it, the crippling frustration that came with it.

I remembered this transition between linear thinking and spiral thinking in engineering. Spiral development and iterative thinking really revolutionized the way we think about design in general and the way we engineer new technology solutions. Since business building is just another exercise in design—designing a business instead of a widget—wouldn't the same methodology apply? Of course it would. The phases of the design spiral are absolutely applicable to the different phases that we go through as business owners to develop new products.

Instead of being driven forward by success, then, we're driven forward by curiosity. Curiosity sprouts naturally out of what we can learn in each step and what lies around the next curve of the spiral. Curiosity manifests as forward motion and growth. Success is a by-product of the process.

Once I made the jump of applying the design spiral to business, it was only a short jump further to apply it to personal development. Isn't life just an exercise in design if you're deliberately creating a life that you love? You go through these phases of inspiration and ideas. You go through phases of implementation and making ideas reality. You go through phases where you're out there testing your ideas or yourself, taking action, and getting things done. You go through phases of reevaluation, rest, and recasting of the vision so that you come around again into the next turn of the spiral. As I looked at my own life, I could certainly see the same phases emerge.

Good design is good design, whether you're designing a new technology, you're building a business, or you're creating a life.

I love the shape of the spiral. It's simple and complex at the same time. It occurs naturally all over nature in the unlikeliest of places. It helps connect disparate parts of a wide-ranging path. It connects us to our own inner journey within as well as our external adventures in the wide world.

Before we can learn how to use the spiral, however, we have to break down some lies we've been telling ourselves. We have to debunk some myths that have been handed down to us. These myths are culturally held paradigms that hold us back from accessing our own natural rhythms because our rhythms are so individually tailored to who we are. We have to break through the cultural status quo to get to new ideas.

Get your sledgehammer. I'll wait.

PART II: MYTHS

CHAPTER FOUR

The Dichotomy Myth

You know those Miller Light commercials from the late 1980s? People got into arguments about a beer that either "tastes great!" or is "less filling!" Comically, after a few rounds of yelling back and forth with increased intensity, the two people shouting these beloved beer qualities at each other would throw down. This occasionally resulted in two beautiful women wrestling in a mud pit, with mildly interested onlookers standing by.

The point of the commercial, of course, was that having a beer that both tastes great and is less filling is totally possible and that these people were arguing for nothing. They promised that Miller Lite was that beer (a dubious claim, but okay). The humor was that the people in this comedy of errors were pitting two concepts against each other that were not mutually exclusive.

Humans love dichotomy, dividing things into two mutually exclusive or opposite parts. It's easier to process the clean lines of "this, not that" than to try to sort out a complex cocktail of qualities. We love to see dichotomy in our external environment (our beer, for example), but we love even more to see dichotomy in ourselves. Dichotomy gives us something to both identify with and identify against, taking "this, not that" to the potent level of "I *am* this, not that."

Think of how many personality or identification frameworks you know that put you somewhere on a spectrum. Myers-Briggs gives you four spectra all at once, contained within a single framework. While each of these qualities is intended to be a continuous spectrum with gradations and degrees of intensity, in the end, we simply get single letters that we love to use to define ourselves. I am an introvert, not an extravert. I am intuitive, not sensing. I am feeling, not thinking. I am judging, not perceiving.

Just reading that, you can see the problem. What rational human being would categorize himself or herself as "feeling, not thinking" or "thinking, not feeling"? These are false dichotomies that take advantage of the human love of a clear line and of labels, but they ultimately don't belong in the mud pit together.

(Can you even imagine it? Can you imagine two beautiful women in a mud pit rolling around comically, screaming at each other, "Sensing!" "Intuitive!" "Sensing!" "Intuitive!" The mind reels.)

We love to set up these dichotomies for ourselves. By extension, they come out in our businesses too. Our heads are filled with voices, usually taking the form of some very influential, highly visible people who are yelling at us and getting ready to throw down.

"You need structure!"

"Go with the flow!"

"Structure!"

"Flow!"

"Structure!"

"Flow!"

It's our inner primitive brain that likes this fight because the primitive brain wants the simplicity of the clean line and the clear label. This, too, is a false dichotomy. Having both structure and flow at the same time in your business is not only possible but beneficial.

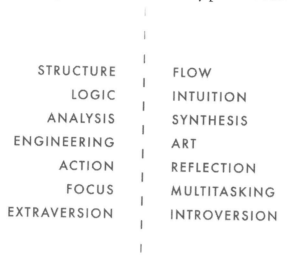

STRUCTURE	FLOW
LOGIC	INTUITION
ANALYSIS	SYNTHESIS
ENGINEERING	ART
ACTION	REFLECTION
FOCUS	MULTITASKING
EXTRAVERSION	INTROVERSION

Dichotomies

Somehow, aligning yourself against something makes it easier to define what you're aligned with. Somehow, saying who you are not and what you do not stand for makes it easier to say who you are and what you do stand for. But in reality, those dichotomies are a myth because as humans, we encompass all of those qualities. Some of them might come out more often than others, but don't kid yourself—they're in there.

These dichotomies aren't hostile sides of a war; they're simply two opposite ends of a spectrum. We encompass the whole spectrum within ourselves. Sure, it's easier to say, "I am this and not that," but that doesn't mean that the black-and-white model actually exists. It's just a mental construct.

Integration means a coming together—not just a meeting at the edges, but a combining. More often than not, integration means a coming together of disparate parts. To look at these parts individually, you might think they would never come together—they seem as unmixable as oil and water. To the casual observer, the two parts merely sit next to each other.

But at the edge where these two separate things meet, there can be unseen hooks. These hooks, like the cuts in a jigsaw puzzle, allow a coming together in harmony and synthesis so that the whole is greater than the sum of the parts.

In our lives, we like to draw lines to keep various parts of ourselves separate from the others. We feel that it's simpler to compartmentalize this way. And it can be simpler to break things down into their smallest known pieces in order to handle overwhelming moments. But what if we were able to find our greatest power—if our whole selves were greater than the sum of our various parts—when we bring all our pieces together in integration?

Structure and Flow

I love structure and flow as a dichotomy because this pair tends to have big emotional connections. Structured thinking is associated with being left brained, whereas going with the flow is associated with being right brained. But these qualities can be polarizing. Since *left-brained* and *right-brained* are associated with a state of being, I find that people tend to identify with one or the other, to associate one of these qualities with their very identity and reject the other as "not me."

But structure and flow actually go together. They're not mutually exclusive. On the contrary, they enable each other and work together to help us manifest something awesome.

As a coach and engineer, my first response to someone struggling with accessing personal power is to introduce structure. Structure is the framework upon which you can hang all sorts of unique beauty. Without the structure of the walls, the art would fall to the ground.

Structure is a solid ship that can help keep you from feeling adrift—help you stop expending the energy of treading water.

When it comes to creating the life that you want, structures are the bones that hold the whole thing together. Structures support stability, predictability, and sustainability. Think those qualities aren't sexy? Think again. Stability, predictability, and sustainability cut out the stress and churn of spinning your tires and enable you to create positive momentum toward your desired steady state.

If you've already put structure in place to cut down stress and churn, you've increased predictability, and in doing so, you've increased stability and sustainability. You've implemented routines, systems, processes, and blueprints. You've drawn maps of your entire life from the mundane to the grand vision.

Then, you progress forward, using your processes and executing the steps you planned out. At some point, the feeling of having it all together may shift into something different. Instead of feeling free to create and impact the world while supported by structure, you feel... hogtied. You feel trapped by the structure that was supposed to liberate you from the everyday mundane to engage in the important work of living your purpose.

What you need more of now is flow.

If life were completely deterministic, then structure would be all you need. You could set up systems and processes that are guaranteed to work every single time in every single circumstance. But life is not deterministic—and thank goodness! It's the messiness, the complexity, the unpredictability, and the unknowns that make life a beautiful adventure. And for these reasons, we need to embrace flow with as much exuberance as we build our structures.

So, while structure surely has its place for providing solid foundations—predictability, stability, and sustainability—getting comfortable with flow is also vital for living in the real, messy, complex, stochastic, unknown world. To stand fixed in this flow and continually fight it is a monumental waste of energy. We must be willing to bend and even move with the flow in order to live efficiently and experience the dynamic spectrum of experience that life has to offer.

To be in flow in business means that you have the empty space to be creative. You have wiggle room. You can breathe free air. Playfulness comes along and helps you access your creative capacity.

To think outside the box, you have to actually get out of the box.

Flow also supports the learning process. When we start out innovating, we don't know everything about what we're trying to do. If we did know everything, the process wouldn't be very innovative, would it? Not only that, but we often don't even know what we don't know. While this might appear to be a scary and even dangerous condition, not knowing what we don't know is part of the fun. It's part of the process of discovery, of problem-solving, of being on the Creator's Journey.

Flow allows us to sit with those unknown unknowns (the things we don't know that we don't know) and imagine new possibilities instead of running screaming from them.

Flow helps us stay open to new ideas and inspirations. These new conceptions can look like brand new ideas and innovations, or they can look like refinements to an existing idea to make it better.

Without flow, we never learn anything new. We never create anything new. We never look at something from a different perspective. We never wonder or get curious or experience the beauty of a lightbulb moment.

Structure provides the framework that creates the empty space needed for flow to happen. It's like the tent poles holding up a circus tent. The structure sets a boundary. It holds a space inside which magic, wonder, and suspension of disbelief can occur. It's really hard (dare I say impossible?) to create magic when you have tent canvas falling down in your face.

In the case of our circus tent, the structure also provides visibility. It signals to everyone around that the circus is in town, and that if they come on down to the tent entrance, they're going to witness some magic. Even if they don't realize what the circus tent is all about from a distance, they can tell that it's something special and that something out of the ordinary is happening. It draws them in.

Healthy structure holds space. It doesn't gratuitously exist. It's there to create the energetic space you need for magic, wonder, innovation, and flow.

Healthy structure holds the big picture. Even if the magic you're creating seems small at first, the structure can hold the space for much bigger magic—the magic you haven't learned yet—so that you can grow into it and not wonder whether or not you have enough space.

Healthy structure is robust. It's not going to collapse or tip over at the slightest breeze or challenge. It's going to stay put and protect that sacred space within.

Healthy structure is visible and distinctive. It's an indicator to those around you that special things are happening here.

Healthy flow is playful, magical, and full of wonder.

Healthy flow is about growth. It's about the learning process. It's about turning the scary unknown unknowns first into known unknowns and then into fully understood knowns. (And once they are knowns, you can actively do something about them.)

Healthy flow is experiential, experimental, and evolutionary.

Healthy flow is not directionless. It can be directed, diverted, manipulated, and pointed in the right direction for purpose.

Healthy flow feels like freedom.

Structure and flow may seem like opposing qualities. It may feel as if you have one and not the other, or even as if you *are* one and not the other. But in reality, you need both in order to thrive. They have a symbiotic relationship. And even if you prefer working with one over the other, you have access to both.

When you can integrate principles of structure and flow, you step into the fullness of your own personal power using all the tools available to you.

Masculine and Feminine

Most of the dichotomies here can actually be boiled down into masculine and feminine energies. Now let me be clear here—masculine and feminine energies have nothing to do with being male or female. Every human possesses both masculine and feminine energies. As we found with structure and flow, you may find that you prefer working with one energy or the other, but don't be fooled—you always have access to both.

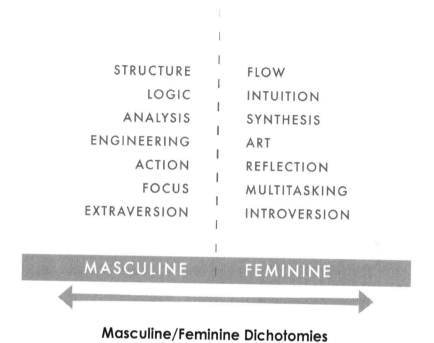

STRUCTURE	FLOW
LOGIC	INTUITION
ANALYSIS	SYNTHESIS
ENGINEERING	ART
ACTION	REFLECTION
FOCUS	MULTITASKING
EXTRAVERSION	INTROVERSION

MASCULINE | FEMININE

Masculine/Feminine Dichotomies

When someone uses the words *masculine* or *feminine*, what images come to mind?

You may start by thinking of cartoonish caricatures of masculinity or femininity. The cartoon masculine may show up as overdeveloped muscles, an insistence on never feeling emotions, very large weapons, and an awkwardness about anything to do with the operation of a household. The cartoon feminine may show up with an impossible hourglass figure, doting and emotional behavior, an interest in superficial pursuits, and a general contentment with working behind the scenes. You can laugh at the images of He-man and Jessica Rabbit that just popped into to your mind, but underneath the silly, exaggerated images lie the toxic masculine and toxic feminine.

When we talk about taking this dichotomy to the extent of toxicity, it's easy to yelp, "That's not what I meant by it!" But it's important to realize where the extremes go, because it reinforces why integration of these polarities is so important.

Healthy masculinity is represented by structure, analysis and logic, process and standardization, an external focus, achievement, milestones, or results-driven motivation. It's focused and streamlined.

Toxic masculinity is represented by these qualities taken to the extreme: rigidity, coldness and ruthlessness, mechanistic or robotic approaches, aggression, compartmentalized and stovepiped thinking, obsession with success and metrics. This is the picture of the larger-than-life business that doesn't seem at all connected to humanity. This is the villain in the monomyth. We love to hate toxic masculinity, and yet we exalt it. We hold our boys to this standard: Can they play in this world? Are they man enough? And we hold our girls to this standard, too.

Toxic masculinity has become a buzzword in this age of feminism rising. Even so, the concept becomes a caricature of itself. We don't seek to understand it or find the thread of what we need inside it. It's painted with broad, uniform strokes: the evil that we battle. And as we're smashing the patriarchy, we not only forget the healthy masculine that helps us get shit done, we also forget the flip side of the coin: the toxic feminine.

Maybe that's too strong a statement. We don't forget that toxic femininity is there because this is the caricature of femininity that has been forced on us culturally throughout generations.

Healthy femininity is represented by collaboration and relationship, rest and rejuvenation, reflection and reevaluation, intuition and internal focus, empty space and flow, creativity and innovation, receptivity, and trans-contextual thinking.

But toxic femininity, as with toxic masculinity, is the composition of these qualities taken to the extreme: irrationality, emotionality, group think, inaction and stagnation, scatter and chaos, unpredictability (and, worse, unreliability), and maybe most of all, a lack of drive.

These are the labels that get put on women—the labels that hold us back.

We need to realize that masculinity and femininity are tools that all humans have access to, regardless of gender presentation or preference. As humans, we contain the whole unto ourselves. It's only when we lose sight of the importance of the other side that we drift into toxicity, and it's the other side that helps pull us back from the edge, back into healthy energetic expressions.

The trouble with this is that in our patriarchal, male-obsessed culture, it's acceptable to say that a woman has healthy, well-developed masculine traits. It is perfectly fine for a woman to claim and nurture her inner masculine energies, even to the point of overdevelopment. She does this in order to fit in and compete and have a seat at the table in male-dominated environments, to the detriment and the loss of her connection to her feminine energy. Her feminine energy should come so innately and effortlessly to her, and yet she actively shuns it, ignores it, and tamps it down.

But it's worse for men. Men are also encouraged to develop their masculine energies, the skills and tools that come so naturally. A heightened focus on these areas slam the masculine aspect up against the wall of the extreme. Conversely, it's culturally unacceptable for a man to have a healthy feminine aspect—even though it is there by virtue of his very humanity. He quickly loses touch with this tempering, balancing, integrative side that allows his natural masculine tendencies to fully shine and bear fruit. Instead, we reduce the feminine presence within men to crying or other uncontrolled displays of emotion.

Men already know that there's a cyclical process by which progress is made. Men already know that empty space is required for true innovation, and the biggest decisions come from the gut, only guided (not defined) by the data. Men already know that the feminine is within them, voiced or not. It's all there under the surface.

There's significant power in naming these energies for what they are and claiming them for our own. The integration of masculine and feminine is the single most powerful thing we can do to feel fulfilled and whole, to truly innovate while creating the sustainability and constancy we crave, and organizationally to allow the whole to be greater than the sum of the parts.

It's all there already. Will you claim it?

CHAPTER FIVE

The Balance Myth

If you've ever done yoga before, you have plenty of experience with balance. While balance seems as though it should be a state of standing still, when you're in a balance pose, your muscles are constantly firing. If you were to look inside your ankle as you stand in a tree pose, all of the little neurons are constantly activating every single little stabilizing muscle. You might appear to be standing still if you're observed from a distance, but from the inside of your own physical experience, you're rocking and rolling all over the place, making constant adjustments, in constant motion. A balance pose in yoga is a myth.

When we talk about dichotomies or sets of seemingly opposing extremes, we like to think about balance between them. Just as the dichotomies themselves are myths, so is balance between the dichotomies. Even if you achieve a state of somehow temporarily coming to rest in between two extreme concepts, the fact is that you're not really standing still. You're in motion. If you're trying to maintain that balanced state, you're going to have to make constant adjustments to maintain that state. Frankly, just as in yoga, that's hard work.

Because I'm a scientist and a nerd (two labels I happily embrace), I like to go back to physics. Physics has so many answers that not only explain the way the universe works on a physical level but also beautifully illustrate life and philosophy.

Consider the physics example of a stable versus an unstable system. A stable system will always return to the point of equilibrium. Picture a valley with a ball inside it. If you disturb the ball and push it up onto one side of the valley, eventually it will come back to equilibrium at the bottom of the valley. Sure, it might oscillate back and forth for a while, but inevitably, gravity and friction will do their work, and the ball will come to rest at the bottom in a stable position. But that's not balance.

Stable System

Balance is more like the reverse situation, the unstable system. If you imagine a hill instead of a valley, and you imagine a little ball sitting on top of the hill, any disturbance to that ball—any disturbance at all—will cause it to roll down one side or the other. In fact, even if you were to attempt this experiment, it's almost impossible to get that ball to stand on top of the hill in the first place. The point where the ball will not roll to one side or the other is so minuscule that it's almost impossible to find in the real world. It's a mathematical anomaly.

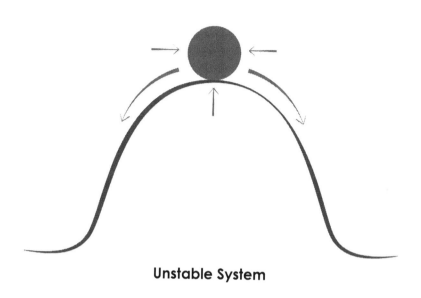

Unstable System

This is balance—an unstable position, a mathematical anomaly. You have to constantly be applying forces to the ball to keep it on top of the hill, pushing the ball back up to the top and holding it there or pushing it to one side as it wants to roll to the other. Balance is not a maintainable state, at least not without a massive expenditure of energy.

Even as we look back at the dichotomies that make us so comfortable, there's no reason to pick just one point between two extremes. At any given moment, more qualities or skills toward one side of the spectrum might serve you better than those at the other side, but that set point is constantly changing. Just as with yoga or the ball on top of the hill, you have to make constant adjustments to find the set point that's right for you at the present time.

When you do find the location of that set point, it's dependent upon a whole bunch of internal/external factors that are extremely personal to you and your specific situation. Before you know it, you'll have to not only make adjustments and fire your energetic muscles to stay in that same place at that set point but also use your muscles and do the work it takes to move the ball to the next set point. Your situation is changing, your needs are changing—therefore, the place where you need to find balance is also changing.

We have a hard time with this as humans. We like to think that our own needs and desires are fixed. It's comforting to think that we can depend on them being constant. We like what we like, and we know what we like. We want what we want, and we know what we want. It feels a bit uncomfortable and unsettling that we might need to move the set point all the time.

In reality, it's healthy and normal and desirable to be in this constant state of motion. Why? Because growth is constant. If your set points aren't changing, it probably means you're not growing.

So how do we deal with this desire for balance? Instead of finding a specific set point—a specific state we call balance—we should be willing to direct our motion in the direction we're aiming for. We should also embrace the fact that at any given moment we might need more of something and less of another. We might need more of one skill and less of another. We might need more of one emotion and less of another. This is beneficial to help us get different jobs done, to help us achieve different goals.

We use the concept of balance to help us navigate the tricky waters of the dichotomies we talked about previously. The dichotomies help us simplify roles and identities with labels (this, not that). And balance is supposed to help us with the dichotomies. But not so fast—the dichotomies are myths, and balance is a myth too.

You contain the fullness of the dichotomy in you, and that means that you have access to all of the tools across the spectrum. You might tend toward being an introvert, but you actually contain the entire spectrum of introversion and extraversion within you. That means you have extravert tools that you can use. And if you always stay balanced on the introvert side of the spectrum, you might never make it over to use those extravert tools. You might never get comfortable with them, learn how to use them to your advantage, and put them into action to make your dreams come true.

There might be times when your balance set point slides over toward the extravert end of the spectrum. Maybe you're at a professional conference or spending the weekend with your best girlfriends. In those moments, it's beneficial and possible to be balanced more toward extraversion. Similarly, there may be times when you need an extra measure of solitude and retreat, and your balance point slides over toward the introvert side even more. Both of these cases are normal, useful, and well within your capability. It doesn't mean you're not balanced. It means your set point is in motion as you grow and access what you need in the present moment.

Instead of thinking of balance as a static state to be achieved, think about balance as motion. Think about it as a dance. A constant giving and receiving, which, interestingly enough, is also moving back and forth between the extremes of a dichotomy. It's inhaling and exhaling.

You don't really balance between inhaling and exhaling. That would be holding your breath. You can do that. You can hold your breath for a minute, maybe two minutes if you're really good at it. You can even hold your breath while you're doing vigorous activity, like swimming underwater. But you would never want to sustain that state of balance; it would be unhealthy. In fact, in the case of breathing, it would be fatal to sustain a balance between inhaling and exhaling.

Instead, you embrace all of the gifts of inhaling when you do it—you accept and receive that nutritious oxygen, that delicious fresh air. And then you accept all of the gifts of exhaling when you do it—releasing all of the carbon dioxide, germs, and toxins that leave your body when you exhale.

You accept that you're not always going to be inhaling. Sometimes you're going to exhale.

And you're not always going to be exhaling. Sometimes you're going to inhale.

You accept that there's a dance between the two. You do this naturally, without thinking about it. You don't beat yourself up for not having balance. You just allow yourself to breathe.

I'm proposing that you reject balance for all dichotomies in a similar way. Fully accept the gifts of each phase of your own cycle. Even though you're completely engaged in one activity that seems like the antithesis of another phase, trust that eventually you'll come around again into the other (opposite) phase. Trust that you'll accept those gifts at that point. You'll release the gifts of your current phase of the cycle when it's time, trusting that you'll eventually return to where you started.

This isn't static balance, this is motion. This is a dance. You have to accept that your state is always changing in order to be healthy, in order to be growing, and in order to create the work you want to create.

We like to think about a vision of life or business as a static snapshot in time. "Oh, if my life just looked like this painting in my head, then I would be happy."

But in reality, we don't crave a static vision of our life. We crave growth. We crave excitement and adventure. And even if you're not the most adventurous person in the world, I'm betting that you crave the subtle ebb and flow of the rhythms of everyday life. Standing still isn't acceptable to you. If standing still isn't acceptable, then balance isn't acceptable either.

And so, I'm going to ask you as we move forward to let go of the idea that what you need is balance. And let go of the idea that your creative vision will manifest as a static snapshot.

Embrace the dance between the dichotomies that you fully embody. Embrace the idea that what you crave is growth, excitement, and the gentle rhythms of motion. And accept that nothing gets created in stagnation. You need to have forward momentum to even start to think about creating something new.

Part of creating forward momentum is letting go of the idea that there's some perfect balance that's going to allow you to achieve it. Allow yourself to dance.

CHAPTER SIX

The Linearity Myth

I already mentioned the Hero's Journey, conceived by Joseph Campbell, which is the framework that underlies nearly all of our human stories. All of the stories we tell in art, literature, theater, and film represent some permutation of the Hero's Journey.

The Hero's Journey is itself an archetype: a simplified caricature of a process to help us understand our own complex, real processes. The players in the Hero's Journey are character archetypes. Archetypes are useful to help us understand ourselves, because they simplify complex reality. But they become limiting or even dangerous if we allow ourselves to believe that reality is that simple.

We tend to set goals as if the path to achieving those goals is a straight line. In a perfect world, you'd start out at point A, make changes, and see progress. You'd move, slowly or quickly, but consistently toward point B. Or would you? Anyone who has ever set any kind of goal knows that moving straight from point A to point B is only very rarely how it actually goes down.

Why do we have such an obsession with linearity? Why do we have this obsession with moving directly between point A and point B on the shortest route possible? Partially, it seems easier to think about that way. Partially, our culture is always in a hurry, regardless of whether there's an actual reason to hurry. It's what our culture throws at us. It's hard to express a rambling, chaotic, or even organized-but-not-linear path in popular culture. When we view a movie or a TV show or read a novel, there might be twists and turns in the plot line, but generally speaking, the plot line starts out at point A and moves along toward point B. It does that very particularly, very strategically, because it follows the path of the Hero's Journey.

When you're on a creative path, whether that means creating a product solution, building a business, or pursuing your own personal creative interests, you're on the Creator's Journey. The Creator's Journey is quite similar to the Hero's Journey because it goes through predictable stages. Along the way, there will be challenges to overcome, and there will be friends and allies. There will be skills picked up along the way so that, ultimately, the creative idea can be birthed.

The Creator's Journey is every home improvement show you've ever watched. All you have to do is tune into HGTV for a few minutes and watch one of those half-hour shows, and you'll see the entirety of the Creator's Journey laid out in front of you. The designers have a vision about how the home could be. They show you the "ordinary world"—the house as it is at the beginning of the journey—very run down, old, falling apart, with out-of-date décor. Then they show the vision for what could be. This is the quest that is being bestowed on the Creator. Drawings and overlays pop up on-screen showing the changes they'll make. They craft a vision for what the kitchen could look like once they've torn out these horrible 1970s-style cabinets and replace them with sleek, minimalist design.

Then, they start work. Along the way, what happens? Inevitably, they run into trouble. There's a crack in the foundation for which they need to supply the extra budget to repair. They need to make a strategic choice about how they spend their budget. They were going to take out a column in the middle of the room and make it a totally open floor plan, but it turns out the column needs to stay there because it's structurally important, so they have to work around it. Drama abounds. For effect, these shows always cut to commercial right when the designer's jaw drops.

Inevitably, though, they solve the challenge and then move to the next thing so that the vision ultimately comes to fruition. At the end of the show, they reveal the new house, how much money they made off of the flip, or the happy family members who have moved into their beautiful new home, utilizing all of the new space they didn't know they had.

This Creator's Journey makes for dramatic home improvement television, but it also plays out in any kind of creative endeavor. You get inspiration to create a vision. The path to go from point A (where you are now) to point B (implementing the vision) seems straightforward. How hard could it be? You just need to write up some code. You just need to create some content. It seems like a straight line.

But embedded in that path are challenges to solve. They're the unknown unknowns, the things you could never have known about when you started out on your Creator's Journey. It's not that you weren't prepared enough. It's not that you didn't think your whole vision through. It's not that your plan wasn't good enough. These challenges, while unknown, are expected. The more you can expect to have challenges that you never would have anticipated, the more prepared you'll be for the Creator's Journey.

Instead of looking at all of these challenges along the way of the Creator's Journey as roadblocks to the linear progress of the journey, look at them as natural iterations of the journey that help you get to the end goal of birthing your creative endeavor. Iterations are opportunities to learn something new that changes everything. Iterations are opportunities to be innovative in a way that's different from what you had initially expected. And this is how we grow.

One of my kids' favorite picture books is *Harold and the Purple Crayon*. Not only do my kids love hearing it, but I love reading it. Because in *Harold and the Purple Crayon*, Harold is a creator, and he's on the Creator's Journey. As the story is being told, the main character, Harold, is actually drawing the illustrations on the page with the purple crayon in his hand. The book is co-created between you (the reader) and Harold (the character).

On the first page of the book, Harold starts out by drawing a long, straight path so that he won't get lost. That's how he begins his journey. But within the first few pages, Harold realizes that he doesn't seem to be getting anywhere on his long, straight path, so he leaves the path for a shortcut across a field.

Everything that happens for rest of the book happens after he leaves the straight path. All of the adventure, all of the learning, all of the fun, all of the wacky hijinks happen after he leaves the long, straight path. There is a lesson for us all here—not just that leaving space for those challenges and iterations is a natural part of the process, but also that the key to adventure and fun—and yes, innovation— lies in embracing a process that doesn't look so linear or predictable.

The story of Harold leaving a long, straight path really spoke to me personally in my own journey because I had set that goal to be an astronaut as a child. I had moved toward that goal in a uniformly linear fashion. From the time I was 12 to the time I was about 28, I had just checked off all of the boxes on the long, straight path, one after the other. I assumed that my career as a professional engineer would take a long, straight path. I could see it all laid out in front of me: climbing the corporate ladder, having all the right experience, shaking all the right hands at all the right times.

When I decided I was going to do something different and create my own destiny in my work, I embarked on my own Creator's Journey. I left the long, straight path behind. That leap felt so scary to me at the time. For the entirety of my life and career, I had been able to see my path stretching out in front of me, and it seemed so dependable, and there was a certain amount of security in it. Leaving the long, straight path felt scary because it was a step off into the unknown.

It took me a while to accept the exhilaration factor of the very opportunity for adventure. I had to get used to the idea that I wasn't constrained by the limits of that long, straight path and that I was now able to co-create the vision of my own Creator's Journey along the way, just like Harold did. The crayon was in my own hand.

The crayon is in *your* hand. Whatever you're focused on creating, the crayon is in your own hand.

Your journey might look like a long, straight path for a while, depending on what you're doing, but human existence as a whole is not linear. Humans are not meant to be linear, robotic beings who follow prescriptive steps. Humans are cyclical beings. Humans move through life in iterations. This is illustrated by the fact that the Hero's Journey and the Creator's Journey at first look like long, straight paths, simply moving from point A to point B. In reality, if you look at the fine details of the archetypal stories, you'll find they include iterations.

That's what creates the drama. That's what creates the challenge. That's why we don't all step into our own creative power—because it's hard to step onto a blank page with just a purple crayon in our hands and trust that the next step will be made known to us.

The fact is that when we expect our creative process to be linear, we're furthering the linearity myth. Yes, it seems simpler for us to think about the process in that linear way, but humans are not linear beings. Humans are inherently cyclical. Women in particular have a physical cycle embedded in their bodies. But just because men don't necessarily have a physical cycle doesn't mean they aren't cyclical beings. We live on the Earth all together, and the Earth is a cyclical place. As the Earth journeys through her seasons, she takes us with her.

Thinking that we should be performing in the same way at all times, to the same level, with the same set of skills coming to the forefront is an illusion. We're not robots. We're messy, organic, evolutionary beings who are always growing, always learning, always changing.

Unfortunately, our post-industrial-revolution culture would like us to believe that we're more robotic than we are. In this world, humans are just interchangeable cogs in the machine of industry that can be counted on to behave in this robotic fashion: always fulfilling the same function, always fulfilling the same levels of performance, always with the same skill set at the forefront, and always emotionally happy to fulfill the exact same duties at the exact same levels in perpetuity.

When cyclical, organic, evolutionary humans are dropped into that industrial, robotic frame of work, there are negative consequences. We get really unhappy. We have emotional fallout. Sometimes we convert our emotional stress into physical stress, and we exhibit physical fallout. We have breakdowns. We get sick because we capture that emotional stress within our physical bodies.

What if we were to embrace nonlinearity? Instead of having our organizations insist on this industrial, robotic treatment of the human component, what if we embraced our cyclical, evolutionary human nature? What if we embraced the need for iteration? What if we embraced that an individual human on a week-to-week basis or month-to-month basis may have different skills coming to the forefront, may have different preferences, may be able to perform at different levels on different tasks? What if we embraced that?

Just as enforcing the linear model causes problems, embracing the cyclical model brings benefits. You, your team, your colleagues, your clients, and your family thrive with cycles. If we don't put linear expectations on our children, if we instead allow them to be cyclical, evolutionary, iterative beings, we're going to see our children thriving and happy and stepping into their true genius with the freedom to explore, to innovate, and to move our whole civilization forward in a way that not only supports our kids as individuals but the whole of humanity as well.

Embracing iteration means more happiness and less stress because people are allowed to be themselves, exactly as they are in the present moment. This is how you're allowed to bring your whole self to work. You can show up exactly as you are. What if you could use the skill set you have right now and right where you are in your cycle at work? What if you allowed yourself to build your business cyclically? What if you didn't need to have the entire path laid out before you and you didn't have to know everything about everything before you even began? What if you allowed it to be iterative? Wouldn't that take a weight off your shoulders?

PART III: THEORY

CHAPTER SEVEN

Spiral Theory

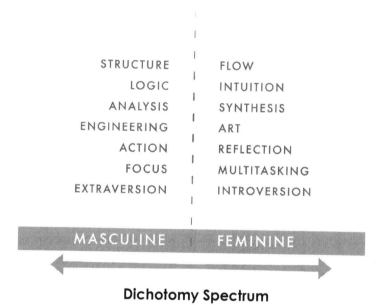

STRUCTURE	FLOW
LOGIC	INTUITION
ANALYSIS	SYNTHESIS
ENGINEERING	ART
ACTION	REFLECTION
FOCUS	MULTITASKING
EXTRAVERSION	INTROVERSION

MASCULINE | FEMININE

Dichotomy Spectrum

THE SPIRAL IS THE ULTIMATE INTEGRATION of all these dichotomies we try so hard to identify with and against.

The spiral is about not only moving back and forth between each set of extremes but also letting them dance together. It is about using the strengths of each phase as they come, accepting that you are this *and* that, not either-or. You have access to all the tools in your toolbox and can use them in a practical way to thrive in all parts of the Creator's Journey, which is the spiral path.

The history of the explicit use of the spiral in a structured way for developing creative projects is rooted in engineering methodology, where I learned it as a practical tool. But as in nature, once you see the spiral emerge in one context, it starts popping up everywhere.

When I was in college, I spent a summer as an intern at Glenn (formerly Lewis) Research Center, a NASA facility located outside Cleveland, Ohio. This particular NASA facility isn't especially glamorous, as some of them can be—you usually won't run into astronauts in the hallway, and you can't accidentally wander into a mission control center for manned or robotic spacecraft. But this was my first opportunity to work with NASA, and I was pumped.

In Cleveland, I was assigned to the National Microgravity Research Center to support the work of a researcher named Dr. Vedha Nayagam. Vedha had a lot of research interests in many different areas—microbiology, neurology, climatology, and microgravity combustion. From the outside, it seemed a little scattered and chaotic, but once I was in Vedha's circle, I started to see this hunger for understanding as a common thread that looped through all of physics—all of existence. I came to know Vedha's research through his work in microgravity combustion behavior—that is, how fire behaves in space. The justification for getting project funding was to say that understanding the way that fire behaves in space can help us design protection systems for astronauts and equipment on long-duration space missions. Sounds important, right? It is, but that project only scratched the surface.

Our little team investigated the combustion behavior of gaseous methane in slow-swirling flows. An incredible, unexpected thing happened when we lit the flames next to a rotating disk. The flames formed spirals. And the flame tips precessed in mandala-like patterns, the same shapes you produce when you play with a Spirograph toy (mathematically known as hypotrochoids and epitrochoids).

Vedha was obsessed with all things spiral. Other areas of his research interest included the patterns of electrical pulses in the human heart (spirals, of course), the formation of weather vortexes around islands (spirals, duh), neurological patterns in brain waves (spirals), patterns in labor contractions during birth (spirals again), and natural spiral formations in nautilus shells and ferns. He wanted to know how it all worked and, most of all, *why* these things all presented the same way with the same math. In his mind, it had to be connected somehow, and he was determined to find the connection.

It was while working with Vedha that I started to see spirals everywhere. At the time, I thought him eccentric and perhaps a little scattered. We were asking questions about what was happening, hoping but not really expecting to figure out *why*. Seeing the patterns emerge was enough for the time being, and knowing that these underlying patterns were important, that any one manifestation of the spiral could hold the key to unlocking the mysteries of another manifestation of the spiral, spurred us on to dive deeper.

I'll admit, it was incredibly frustrating, as a 20-year-old, to be working on this spiral research and not have an answer to the "why do we even care about this" question. Which is why, when I learned about Spiral Development as a design methodology, I got along with it so well. Here was a practical application of the spiral that I could actually use to get something done.

Spiral development methodology in engineering design was born out of a reaction to the unwieldy and expensive expectation that developing a new technological solution should be a straightforward, linear process. First you understand what you need to design, then you design a solution, test it, and—wha-bam! You have a new innovative widget that solves all your problems. As you've seen, this is known as the Waterfall method, because your project progress trips along the path, like so much water cascading down a river bed on a hillside. If only innovation were that clean and simple.

Unfortunately, not only is the creative, innovative process inherently messy, organic, and evolutionary, insisting that it's clean, simple, and linear has real consequences. If you learn something new about how you can or can't use your ideas in your design project late in this linear development cycle, at best, it's really expensive to fix it and, at worst, it's catastrophic to the project. So, in the mid-1980s, as computer technology innovation surged, engineers rebelled against the rigid, ridiculous processes that backed them into impossible corners. Instead, they embraced the organic, evolutionary nature of design and developed new paradigms like Iterative, Agile, and Spiral Development.

The linear, or Waterfall, method is a rather brute-force style of creating something new. It's not that it can't be done—it can. It just takes a whole lot of money, manpower, and commitment. It's the "get a bigger hammer" approach.

My very first engineering internship was in a small research and development (R&D) machine shop, designing and building paint-mixing equipment for automotive and aircraft refinishing. It was pretty fun—I got to learn how to use all the machine shop tools, and I would end the day happily coated in machine grease. I loved the feeling of working with my hands, of forming and cutting the sheet metal, the tubing, the gears to suit my needs, and then assembling all the little piece-parts into some whole unit that actually worked, humming away for some higher purpose. My manager for those summers used to chuckle when I'd get him to help me figure out how to make pieces fit together that just wouldn't, despite having been measured twice (or, let's be honest, thrice) and cut once. He'd just smile and say, "Time to get a bigger hammer." I distinctly remember a device that I'd designed entirely on my own. One corner of it wouldn't come together in alignment, and he grinned in satisfaction when he thwacked the side of my little device with a rubber mallet and it popped into place.

There's definitely a time and a place to use the tools in your toolbox to nudge a small corner into alignment. The trouble is that sometimes the Waterfall method backs us into a corner we can't get out of. We start out and assume that we'll just walk right through the process—design, manufacture, assemble, test, deploy—and then we'll be done. I certainly expected that my little device would just slide right together, that all the bolt holes would align the first time, and that the motor would come on when I flipped the switch. The fact that the corner didn't fit together came out of the blue. It hadn't even entered my consciousness that the parts might not fit together the first time, after I had planned and measured so carefully. I was mad. I was swearing at the thing.

I didn't give myself time or patience to go back and think about how the design could be better or how I could make it easier to assemble. I just kept banging my head against the same old wall of "I designed this to fit together. Why won't it go?!" In this case, it turned out to be salvageable. A tap with a hammer got it to click into place. But what if it hadn't? I would have been going back to the drawing board—and doing it with a bad attitude.

Going back to the drawing board isn't necessarily a bad thing. Sometimes it's necessary to refine a design, to incorporate learning that came along the way. Going back to the drawing board is in some ways inherent to the iterative design process—it's just what you do when you allow the process to be iterative. But there are a few key differences between healthy backtracking and what I would have experienced that day.

First, allow yourself the possibility of going back to the drawing board, and be okay with that. During my design exercise, I didn't anticipate having to go back to the drawing board. I thought I was just going to design, build, and present my solution. One, two, three. When my expectation didn't manifest, I was mad. Mad at the hardware, mad at myself, mad at the situation. And it caused me a lot of stress when it really shouldn't have.

Second, if you anticipate that the process will be iterative, you can help yourself not have to go all the way back to the drawing board. You'll probably be able to identify the areas where iteration will help the most, and if you can design flexibility around these specific areas, you can focus the learning process on those areas. If I'd recognized that the bolt-hole alignment of my little device was going to be both tricky and critical to my success, I could have cut the holes bigger, or cut a forgiving slot instead of a hole, or provided myself with an easy way to punch a new hole even once the piece had been formed. This would have caused a lot less heartache than having to scrap a whole pile of sheet metal and remake the entire device from scratch.

The biggest problem with the Waterfall method is that you're assuming you (and the customer) have all the answers about the final outcome up front. While on rare occasions you may be crystal clear about all the details before you ever begin, in most cases there is an evolutionary growth that happens over the course of the project. There needs to be space within the process to accommodate that new awareness, new learning, and new growth.

In addition to assuming that you have complete knowledge of the problem and solution up front, the linear method assumes that the problem and the requirements for the solution are articulated clearly the first time. But that's not reality. Too often, communication of needs can feel like a game of "telephone," with all the people in the process hearing something slightly (or significantly) different to suit their own experience, expertise, and worldview.

As I delved into my own business design after leaving my corporate job for entrepreneurship, I quickly saw the parallels between the engineering design process and the business design process. I was still designing solutions, after all, but instead of designing spacecraft or paint-mixing equipment or any other kind of technical solution, I was designing a business structure. In the end, designing information products isn't so different from designing widgets—good design is good design. It was easy to see how, as a business owner, I was falling into the trap of expecting a long, straight, linear path toward a final product.

It goes back to our initial set of assertions. You are a creator. Whether you're creating spacecraft or software or a service-based business or simply a life that you love, you are a creator. And the creative process is fundamentally nonlinear.

The creative process is iterative.

This is what the engineering community came to in the 1980s. The brute-force, linear method wasn't working. There had to be learning, evolution, and reflection built into the process.

Enter spiral development.

We talked about the phases of the engineering development spiral in Chapter Three. They are, more or less, the steps of the linear, Waterfall development process arranged around the circle with the expectation of iteration: Ideation, Implementation, Testing, and Evaluation.

IMPLEMENTATION   IDEATION

TESTING   EVALUATION

Engineering Spiral

It's not a huge leap to take these phases of an iterative engineering process and apply them more generally to any creative process. And that's what we'll talk about next—how to use this proven, time-tested engineering design methodology to help you with whatever it is you are creating: technical or nontechnical products or solutions, a business that lights you up and changes the world, or the life of your dreams. All of these, as we've established, are acts of radical creativity and innovation, and all are subject to the fundamental principles of creation.

The spiral phases that we'll work with are as follows:

1. **Introspection**: Craft or tune up a vision that's reflective of who you want to *be* and what you want to *do*. Come into stillness with yourself, your team, and your tribe. Ask what's needed and how you can help. Ask yourself what you really want. Look at the big picture of what you're trying to create. Set a course for joy.

2. **Inspiration**: Decide what to do. Decide what problem you're solving and what your general approach to solving it is. If you've already iterated on a problem once or a few times, this step is about taking what you just learned and deciding what to do *next*. This is where the magic, the innovative part of the process happens. This is brainstorming, where the crazy ideas are the best ones.

3. **Implementation**: Build the solution. Depending on where you are in your iterations, this could look like a sketch on a bar napkin, a prototype, or a full-up, ready-to-launch spacecraft. But here's where you birth ideas into physical reality. Note that this period of creation isn't really where the innovation happens (that was Inspiration). Implementation is all about action and physical manifestation.

4. **Investigation**: Test the solution. Get your solution in front of actual people who might use it. Try it on for size. Find out what works and what doesn't. Find out what works *for you* and what doesn't.

1. **(Next Spiral) Introspection (again)**: Pause, reflect, and reevaluate. Take a step back and assess what just happened. Take what you just learned, and think about how you want it to be the same or different in the future. Put this little slice of learning back into the tapestry of the big picture, and figure out if you're still on the path you thought you were on— or if you're on a different adventure. And continue on the spiral path...

IMPLEMENTATION   INSPIRATION

INVESTIGATION   INTROSPECTION

Creative Spiral

The spiral is a fluctuation between the dichotomies that seem to be in opposition: action-taking and reflection; focus and big-picture thinking; structure and flow. But if you take a step back from that granularity and look at the bigger picture, this creative spiral isn't just a creative process adapted from engineering. This creative spiral is an echo of every other cyclical process in our world.

The Earth cycles through seasons: winter, spring, summer, and autumn. The Moon cycles through phases: new, waxing, full, and waning. A woman's body physically cycles through menstrual, follicular, ovulatory, and luteal phases as she prepares for the potential creation of a human being. A woman's life archetypally cycles through maiden, mother (or creatrix), queen, and sage phases. All these cycles are echoes of each other, the rhythms that humans are attuned to as citizens of Earth and children of women. And the creative spiral is no different. Each of these four phased cycles provide a roadmap to help us further understand the phases of the creative process, how we connect with them, and how we can use them.

IMPLEMENTATION
- Summer
- Full Moon
- Ovulation
- Mother (Creatrix)
- Fire

INSPIRATION
- Spring
- Waxing Quarter
- Follicular Phase
- Maiden
- Air

INVESTIGATION
- Autumn
- Waning Quarter
- Luteal Phase
- Queen
- Water

INTROSPECTION
- Winter
- New Moon
- Menstruation
- Sage
- Earth

Spiral with Archetypal Representation

By the way, gentlemen, you are not off the hook here. Women are particularly tuned into cyclical processes because we physically, viscerally connect to cycles. But you, my friend, are also connected to these cycles as a denizen of Earth and the child of a woman. They're in you too, even if you are in total denial about that. I'm hoping that pointing these cycle phases out to you and talking about it will help you not only understand it a little more but also tap into it and harness its power. I hope you can see these phases come out in your own work and life, see how they connect to the bigger picture of humanity, and see that you aren't alone.

From this big-picture—dare I say universal—view of the creative spiral, you can dive down and see the other dichotomies that are dancing within this spiral.

The spiral is a dance between

- Extraversion and introversion

- Isolation and collaboration

- Inspiration/intuition and analytics/logic

- Detail focus and big-picture vision

Perhaps we could sum up the spiral as a dance between masculine and feminine energies.

Every human contains both masculine and feminine energies, regardless of gender. While women might have easier access to their feminine energies, they also have the capability to tap into and powerfully leverage their inner masculine energy. Usually this happens as part of the Implementation and Investigation phases, when the focus is outward, analytical, logistical, data oriented, and action taking.

Similarly, men might have easier access to their masculine energies, but they have the capability to tap into and powerfully leverage their inner feminine energy. This manifests in the creative spiral most often in the Introspection and Inspiration phases, when the focus is inward, reflective, recharging, inspired, disruptively innovative, unique, and artistic.

Embracing Cycles

The spiral cycles are there whether or not you actively engage with them. I can't tell you how many times I've been in the middle of tearing out my hair about my lack of progress or consternation about what do to next, and my coach has said, "Wait—where are you in the spiral right now?" And I sit back and say, "Oh crap, I'm exactly where I'm supposed to be!" And all that consternation melts away. Yes, I'm the one who conceived of the spiral and adapted it for business building, and yet I need to be reminded by my amazing coaches who use my spiral to cut to the chase. (I was going to say, "They use my spiral against me." I love you guys!)

It happens with my coaching clients too. For some reason, the grass always seems greener on the other side of the spiral. One client came to me and said, "I feel like I have tunnel vision! There are *so many* things I need to be working on right now, but I'm only inspired to work in my group." A few weeks later, she came back and said, "I'm multitasking way too much right now! I'm getting all of these little tasks done, but I'm not able to focus on any one thing. Why do I feel so scattered?"

Can you see her conundrum? The spiral fluctuates back and forth between single-minded creative focus, and distributed multitasking. These two states of being are just normal parts of moving through the spiral. I told her, "I'll bet in a couple weeks you'll find that single focus again, but you might feel like you aren't getting 'enough' done again." I wondered what would happen for her if, instead of lamenting that she didn't have the gifts of the opposite part of the spiral, she fully embraced (and worked the hell out of) the gifts of the part of the spiral that she was currently engaged in. What would happen if *you* fully embraced where you are and had faith that the other gifts will come around again as part of your natural creative cycle, without having to force anything?

Alternatively, you can deliberately plan to move from phase to phase of the spiral. You can develop entrance and exit criteria. You can make it very rigorous and very purposeful. The spiral is certainly a solid model for moving through the design process with intention. But even if you're not intentional, the spiral is still there, thrumming your own natural rhythm of creation like a heartbeat.

The spiral represents the Creator's Journey that we all embark on when we bring something new into the world. But even beyond that, the spiral represents the human journey we're all on. It's a journey represented in the turn of the seasons, the waxing and waning of the moon, and the ebb and flow of a woman's womb. This cyclical approach brings a highly feminine energy into a realm that's traditionally very masculine. Even though creative life force is a feminine aspect, engineering and architecture are masculine-dominated fields. The design spiral is in there, part of engineering itself, developed and used by men, and yet the spiral is an ancient symbol of the sacred feminine. It's an ancient symbol of the path that women walk physically and emotionally. This epic human journey we're on together is a story of creation. So creativity, design, innovation—these aren't just career paths or hobbies. This is the very stuff of life.

It's culturally acceptable for women to have enhanced, hyperdeveloped masculine energies. Girls can be tomboys and be into sports, trucks, and science. Women can be in science, technology, engineering, and math (STEM) professions, or climbing the corporate ladder. And though there are still stigmas associated with these preferences and glass ceilings to break, it's still acceptable for them to be doing these things. I see this even in my coaching clients. It's easy to talk to women about their masculine energies, qualities, and aspects. We can talk about drive and self-motivation, analysis and rationality, structure and reliability.

But I have a very hard time talking to male clients about their feminine energies, qualities, and aspects. It feels funny to even say that out loud or type it out on the page. But we need to talk with men about cycles, about rest and reevaluation, about collaboration and relationship, about receptivity and paying attention, about tending the creative flame with empty space and openness.

It's also not culturally acceptable for men to talk about their feminine energies, even as they need and crave them. Indeed, both masculine and feminine energies come together to make us whole humans. They're two sides of our human coin.

Why, if these masculine and feminine aspects are always inside of each of us, do we need to label them? Because naming them gives them power. Naming them gives them equal seats at the table. Naming them raises our awareness that to be truly powerful, we must allow ourselves to play with both energies. And once we get to that place where we can be aware of these two sides at play—not opposing each other in battle but frolicking and playing in a push and pull that only serves to make us stronger, more creative, more prolific than we ever thought possible—once we get to that place of awareness, of admittance, of acceptance, only *then* can we leverage the power of integrating the two.

The spiral is a constant flux between these two sides of ourselves, a constant shifting to adapt to our needs, our environment, our own physical and emotional states. The cycles exist. Are you going to use them to your best advantage or not?

To choose to continue in denial of the power at your fingertips is to leave money on the table. Figuratively but also literally. Ignoring one or the other of these energies as an entrepreneur means you're not leveraging all of the tools at your fingertips to grow a profitable, successful, sustainable venture.

Here's the thing about cycles and flows—you can work with them or against them. When sailing, you can either set your sails with the wind, or you can tack against the wind. Either method will get you somewhere, but one takes a heck of a lot less energy. "But what if the wind isn't blowing in the direction I want to go?" I hear you cry. Well, I may ask why you're fighting so hard. Have you stopped to ask why the wind is blowing in this other direction? Is something there waiting for you that's beyond what you thought possible? Consider whether the wind is actually delivering everything you've been asking for, even if it looks a little different or if the *how* is at odds with what you imagined. You'll make progress either way. But one way is a lot more exhausting and discouraging than the other. One way *feels* like a lot more progress than the other. So, do you want to embrace the cycle or fight against it every step of the way? Do you want to put your energy into fighting or into creating your world-changing work?

There are a lot of women who try to fight their menstrual cycles. They medicate them. They continue with their to-do list as if nothing were different for them and their bodies. They operate at the same level doing the same activities day in and day out without regard to the complex cocktail of hormones adjusting which parts of their brain are being activated. These women end up with "symptoms"—sometimes small, irritating ones and sometimes horrific ones. Cramps, migraines, vertigo, fatigue, constipation—I've been there. And those are just the physical effects, which can be easier to pinpoint than the emotional effects: emotional amplitude, sadness, irritability, even dysphoria.

When a woman not only accepts but *embraces* her menstrual cycle, the symptoms may start to fade. I'm not saying that simply embracing her menstrual cycle is the magic pill to curing all of the very real pain that can come along with it, but it's certainly a start. Once she tunes in to her cycle, she starts to see each phase of it as sacred in its own way. Each cycle phase has its own gifts and tools that are important to her personal functioning and growth.

And so it is with creative cycles. You can fight against them, feel resistance, wrestle with writer's block, and launch to the sound of crickets. Or you can accept or even *embrace* the creative cycles. You can view each phase as important, vital, even sacred to the transformational work of creating something new. Of birthing something into the world. (And I've got news for you—whether you are male or female, you are birthing.) When you yield to the creative cycle, some of the stress goes away. There's context for the creative struggle. Yielding to the gifts of each phase brings a sense of ease. The path forward is a little clearer because you know where you're headed next.

CHAPTER EIGHT

Spiral Phases

THE SPIRAL IS BOTH A PORTAL TO UNDERSTANDING yourself and a method for bringing your creative work into the world. It's a framework you can use to move yourself through your creative process to make it more efficient and effective.

Let's walk through the spiral phases individually and talk about how to know when you're in each phase, how to use the gifts of each phase, and how to know when it's time to move forward. We'll take a look at the engineering design process to ground each phase firmly in the design mindset. We'll also discuss some of the archetypes and imagery that can help us better tap into the energy and gifts of each spiral phase.

Discovery and Progress Spirals

Any creative endeavor, whether a project, a business, or a life by design, can take multiple spirals to develop. Every spiral along the way has the same four phases, but each spiral can take on a different flavor depending on where you are in the development journey. For now, we'll differentiate between your very first time around the spiral (the Discovery Spiral) and subsequent trips around the spiral

(Progress Spirals). Later on, we'll break down the progression of spirals even further as we discuss exactly how they help you grow in knowledge as you move through the spiral vortex.

The Discovery Spiral is significantly different from subsequent spirals because it's about exploring possibilities and unlocking the mystery of what you are trying to create. It's all about self-discovery, about how you work, about your team, about what you really want, about what's really good for you, about what problem you're really trying to solve, and about how you're going to innovate to solve that problem. The Discovery Spiral is exploratory, magical, and chock-full of possibility.

Now, the rest of the spirals that come after, which I call Progress Spirals, have a totally different kind of magic. Instead of discovery magic, they have the magic of making things happen. Progress Spirals build on each other to move you forward on your creative journey, to help you evolve as a human or as an organization, and to help you level up.

The spirals, all strung together, form the Creator's Journey. It's not a linear path from point A to point B, but an ever-evolving, meandering adventure. It may seem aimless if you don't know the signposts to look for, but it actually meanders in a predictable way, in the same way that the Earth progresses through the seasons of the year. Earth changes from year to year, for sure, but within the year, the seasons provide predictable structure.

How do you leverage the beautiful energy of each spiral phase, each season, so that you're making progress, even if it doesn't look like traditional progress such as ticking off boxes or achieving accomplishments? Success and progress look different for each of the phases, so let's talk about what that means. Let's figure out how we can put that progress to good use so that, instead of fighting against the energy of the spiral you're in, you can use it to your advantage.

I personally find when I'm in a period of emotional stress or a feeling of extreme "stuckness," it's usually because I'm fighting the phase of the spiral that I'm in and not allowing it to flow. When that happens, I have to pause, become really present, and think about where I am in the spiral. I use a combination of energies, emotions, and stressors in the present moment to identify where I am. Most of the time, just identifying my current spiral phase helps me feel better because I realize that the gifts of the current phase are available. I'm oriented in my own creative journey. If my consternation is coming from fighting the current phase, it's easy to take a deep breath, calm down, and accept where I am. If my consternation is coming from a deeper place in my intuition, where my inner knowing is whispering that I need to make a significant change, I know that the spiral will naturally come around to a phase where I can enact that change because evolution is built in.

So where do we start? It's an infinite spiral with no beginning or end. How are we going to begin our discussion, our journey? Like any cyclical process, it's a chicken-and-egg problem. The chicken-and-egg conundrum is, of course, based on the life *cycle* of a chicken. We say that the chicken starts in the egg, but really it was the hen that laid the egg prior to the hatching that allowed the egg to be laid and then to hatch. So, which came first? The chicken or the egg? There's a similar cycle with plants. Which came first, the seed or the flower? Do you plant the seed first? Or was there a flower that was pollinated that then made the seed so that the seed could be planted to make another flower?

Instead of getting all existential on you here (don't worry, we'll get to existentialism later), let's just say that if you're the gardener and you want to start a beautiful garden, what's the first thing you're going to go out and get? You're probably going to get seeds. Let's start in the seed phase of your creative process.

The seed phase of a flower is a descent into the dark. When you plant a seed, you put it into the earth, which may look bare or even dead. The seed goes down into the darkness and the quiet. Down there in the darkness, in the muck, the seed germinates, pulls in the nutrients from the earth around it, and begins to sprout. Only after it begins to sprout does it emerge into the light of day. So, let's start in the spiral phase of darkness and quiet to see what sprouts.

CHAPTER NINE

Introspection

WHEN WE PRACTICE YOGA, we do the poses and asanas, the movements and stretches. We deliberately use our breath to our best advantage. We challenge our bodies with exercise, balance, and flexibility, but we end every practice in Savasana, in stillness. Savasana is the counteraction to all of the motion and all of the physical challenge that just happened. It's the opportunity to appreciate your body—everything it just did, everything it's capable of, and everything it's learning how to do. This appreciation is done in quiet, in stillness. The body rests, with no expectation or demand, totally supported by the Earth.

The Introspection phase is the Savasana of the creative spiral.

We're going to start here, and we'll end here as well. This Introspection, this Savasana, opens and closes the spiral cycle.

The Introspection phase has the energy of rest, of retreat, of taking a step back. This phase has the energy of the darkness. It's the energy of percolation, preparation, germination. This is where we ultimately integrate everything we've learned, not just in the last spirals but in the whole of our experience. We gather up our body of knowledge. We integrate the new things we've discovered so we can move forward and create something new. This phase is the preparation for the creation that's about to happen next.

It is a time to step back. It's a time to turn inward. This phase is an introverted phase, a receptive phase, a feminine phase. It's a yin phase.

Introspection is focused on *being* rather than *doing*. This phase is sitting still, listening, and letting the answers come to you. This is listening to your still, small voice—your higher self, your deep intuition. This is taking a break. It's taking stock. It's being open to making changes. This is the opportunity to be adaptive—to redirect, to shape the path, to course-correct. This is the opportunity to celebrate, to give yourself acknowledgment for what you've accomplished, for letting everything that you've done be enough.

This is a phase that's a little calmer, a little quieter, and maybe a little slower than the others. It can feel stable and grounded and solid.

If you're expecting to be somewhere different, this phase can also feel as if you're stuck, as if you've lost all of your momentum. That's the shadow side of the Introspection phase. But make no mistake. It's not stuckness, but a pause that's very desperately needed.

The Engineering Process

In the engineering design process, the Introspection, or Evaluation, phase is extremely important. It's a lot easier (and more cost effective) to fix mistakes or make changes in early phases of project and product development than it is later, when something's about to be deployed. Since the evaluation phase is a more cerebral, thinking time than an action-oriented, building time, this is the ideal opportunity to make adjustments, to allow for change, to make space for evolution in the process.

In the Discovery Spiral, our Introspection objective is to define what it is we're trying to do in the first place. In the case of engineering design, if we were building a new spacecraft, the Discovery Spiral is the time to define what the mission is. We're talking about what we're trying to accomplish and the general scope of the problem, such as how many astronauts it accommodates, how far it has to go, and how long it has to last. These are big decisions that shape the big-picture vision of the project.

After you've traveled the spiral at least one time and you've started to move down the creative path, you come back around into Introspection. You have a chance to incorporate what has just happened during the previous spiral. You have the chance to make changes and consider lessons learned, whether your prototype worked out the way you'd thought it would or not. Introspection allows you the opportunity to analyze what happened, troubleshoot, take the data that you collected and step back from the action. It creates the space to incorporate learning and make a strategic decision about what to do next.

Introspection is also a great time in the engineering process to bring the team together for a big meeting, like a technical design review. A lot of engineers like to complain about design reviews. They complain that nothing is actually getting done. Maybe they think it's just a lot of back-patting. Maybe they think it's a lot of whip cracking or finger-pointing about what's not getting done. But that pause to bring the whole team together in stillness and quiet without all of the action of getting stuff done is critical. To talk about the team's accomplishments, to celebrate the team's successes, to celebrate the milestones met, to then troubleshoot and correct the things that aren't going well, and to understand how we can move forward in spite of that—that's the heart of Introspection.

Seasonal Archetype: Winter

The seasonal archetype for the Introspection phase is winter. When Earth is in its winter season and the sun hangs low on the horizon, the days are short and the darkness of night is long. It's a time of retreat. The trees pull their sap down into their trunks, hunkering down for the winter. Bears retreat into their caves and hibernate. The leaves have fallen, and everything appears dead or, at the very least, asleep. It's dark. Does this sound familiar?

Gardeners plant bulbs in the early days of winter so they can germinate in the earth in the cold darkness, unbeknownst to all of us, and prepare for the spring to come again. Even as I'm writing this chapter, it's winter here in Colorado. My conscious mind has resisted the pull back into rest and rejuvenation, into darkness and stillness, because I consciously want to *do things*. But my body and my spirit are craving the rest, and I know that if I push through it instead of heeding it, I'll end up sick because my system will be out of alignment with where I need to be right now.

If you think about the Introspection phase of your creative process as winter, as a time of retreat, to snuggle up, to come inside, and to prepare for what's coming, that's a good way to tune into the energy of Introspection. Savasana for us, Savasana for Earth.

Elemental Archetype: Earth

The elemental archetype associated with the Introspection phase of the spiral is Earth. Earth as an archetype represents solidity and stability. It represents groundedness and stillness.

On a personal level, it's a good time to reconnect with your body and pay more attention to physical self-care. For a business, organization, or project, it's a good time to take a look at infrastructure and logistics—the foundational elements that make the rest of the creative process possible. You can't grow a flower without the soil, and the soil provides the infrastructure for the rest of the growth cycle to happen.

Plant life isn't directly part of the soil. The life is in the seed, but the seed can't develop into a flower without the soil to support it. Again, we're in Savasana, where our bodies are supported by the Earth.

It's the time to ask, "Do I have the support I need to move my business forward? Do I have the support in my personal life to grow into the person I'm meant to be?"

That is what the Earth archetype represents.

How Do You Know You're in the Introspection Phase?

When you're settling into Introspection, you might feel your motion slowing down or even grinding to a halt. Physically, you might want to sleep more. You might find that you're needing more rest. You have a lower energy level. You might feel like asking big-picture, open-ended questions. You may feel the pull to take a step back and look at the big-picture vision as opposed to the details of execution.

Sometimes, this is a pleasant sensation. Perhaps you've just come out of a time of action, motion, production, and extraversion—and with it, stress and chaos. Coming down into this period of rest, support, and stillness may feel really good. However, in a culture that values externally visible measures of progress, coming into stillness, rest, and darkness feels like losing momentum. Feeling that momentum seep away can feel like more than stopping. It can feel like taking a step backwards.

I can't stress enough how important it is to heed these impulses to rest, to retreat, to turn inward! In your cyclical creative journey, you'll naturally fluctuate between the big picture and details.

This is your opportunity to look at the big picture. Listen to your body and to your intuition telling you it's time to take that step back. Pause. Come into stillness. Enjoy the darkness. Allow yourself to rest. Seek out gentle, supportive community, without having to be putting yourself out there and performing. It's necessary to give yourself this time to spend with the big picture because, as you progress through more detail-oriented phases of the spiral, you'll keep moving forward toward that big-picture vision.

Introspection is a touchpoint that keeps you grounded in your vision and sets you free to experiment, explore, and implement ideas during other phases.

I find that the harder I fight against the resting, rejuvenating energy of Introspection, the more physical consequences I experience. I get sick. I get irritable and cranky with everybody around me. These are very real consequences of fighting against a phase that you're in instead of easing into the flow of the natural spiral.

How Do You Leverage the Energy and Gifts of Introspection?

On the initial Discovery Spiral, when you're in the Introspection phase, no matter what type of creative journey you're on, your job is to craft the vision.

The vision that you craft in the Discovery Spiral doesn't have to be complete or final. Once the initial vision is crafted, no matter how sparsely, you can move forward and iterate as you learn more in subsequent spirals. Allow yourself the space to explore. You'll have the chance to come back around again and adjust the vision (or change it completely!) on the next Evaluation spiral. But it's so much easier to enact change in a dynamic system than in a static one.

Imagine that you're in a car that's not moving forward and you try to turn the steering wheel. It's difficult to change the angle of the wheels when the car is standing still. You have to put some elbow grease into it to overcome static friction. Static friction is stronger than dynamic friction. Which is why, when the car is moving forward, it feels effortless to turn the wheel. And because it feels effortless, you're able to elicit much finer control even as you expend a lot less energy. It's the same with realizing a vision. It's much easier to change your course when you're moving forward than when you're standing still.

So, make it your objective in the Discovery Spiral to craft a vision, and then begin to take action. Begin to create motion. And trust that it'll be easier to make adjustments from a place of momentum when you come around again.

For product development in the Discovery Spiral, set the end goal and ask the following:

- What is the thing that I am creating? What is the heart of it?

- How does this product reflect my values?

- How does this product meet the needs of the person who's going to use it or buy it or see it?

- How is this product going to speak to me?

- How is this product going to speak to others?

- What do I need to express right now through this product?

For business development in the Discovery Spiral, it's time to ask the big questions about how your work fits in with your life and meets your needs as well as how it broadly serves the world. It's time to ask the following questions:

- How does my business or organization meet the needs of its clients?

- What are the values that are important for my organization?

- What's the strategic vision for the business? Where am I headed?

- Who do I want to be?

- Who do I want to be known as?

- What do I want to be known for?

- What do I want to be offering? What am I putting out into the world as an organization, as a business?

For personal development in the Discovery Spiral, it's going to be about crafting a vision for your life. You want to understand yourself from all different perspectives: physical, intellectual, creative, and spiritual. You have to understand your passions, your desires, and your values. Ask yourself the following:

- How can I live in alignment with my core values?

- What brings me joy?

- How can I avoid or minimize stress?

- Who do I want to be?

- What do I want to do?

- What best supports me, the people I care about, and the causes I care about?

Even though your crafted vision is at a high, big-picture level, feel free to get down into the specifics, when they come to you. The specifics provide focus for your path forward. Even if you don't know exactly how you're going to implement the specifics, you're giving yourself a target to move toward. Filling in the gaps and allowing those specifics to come into their own is the work of the spiral.

For any subsequent Progress Spiral, you'll be coming into Introspection from the Investigation phase. You have put out something out into the world. You have been executing your vision. You have implemented. You have some data to look at to help you see how it's going for you, for your clients, for anybody who's interacting with the vision. And now, armed with some fresh knowledge, you're ready to come back into Introspection.

Generally, during the Progress Spirals, there are two different segments to the Introspection phase.

The first segment is the pause. It's Savasana. It's stillness, retreat, and rest. It's the break from the action that you very much need. You've come around the curve of the spiral from making things happen. You've been outgoing. You've been extraverted. You've been taking action. You've been implementing like crazy. You've been way "out there," but now you're coming back in. The first thing I want you to do is carve out time to rest.

Rest looks different for everybody and every situation. If you're talking about moving a project forward, the rest might be taking the day or a weekend off. If you're creating your work or a business, it might be a retreat or a vacation. If you're creating your dream life, this withdrawal, this turning inwards, could last a long time—a month, six weeks, six months...maybe more. It depends on many factors: how hard you've been pushing, how outside of your comfort zone you've been, how well you've been taking care of yourself along the way.

Don't be afraid to take the time you need. Don't assume some certain prescriptive amount of time is enough. You might need so much more than that. I don't say this lightly because I'm notorious for telling myself up front how much time I'm "allowed" to have off. Sometimes it's super generous—"We're going to take the whole week off, Amy!" But even though it might feel generous at the outset, if it turns out to not be enough, I end up beating myself up for needing more rest. Don't do that. It's taken me a lot of inner work to give myself the grace to serve my own needs for rest, and I'm the better for it. I'm better in all of my roles—wife, mother, business owner, and all-around human being—when I get to rest and recharge.

The first part of this Introspection phase is to come into stillness, turn inwards, and get grounded in the present moment. Attend to your own physical needs. This is true for any creative path—a creative life path, a creative work path, or a creative project path. Take the time to take a break. Create some empty space for yourself and your team. Remember, the seed can't grow without the support of the earth around it, so allow yourself to sink in.

The second segment of the Introspection phase is evaluation. Take stock. This is still low-key and quiet. This doesn't come with the intention to take action, at least not right now. This is a good time to ask yourself questions so that you can integrate what you learned in the previous spiral, including any data you may have gathered.

If you collected data about how things went in the previous Investigation phase, you now have some quantitative proof of what went well and what didn't. You can take that and move forward and make adjustments from it. You can also qualitatively make an intuitive assessment of how things went and how you feel about moving forward.

Evaluation is really about the quantitative and the qualitative coming together. It's the integration of thinking and feeling, of logic and intuition. This is actually one of those edges where you're going to see the integration of masculine and feminine energies. The Introspection phase carries a predominately yin, or feminine, energy. But within the phase, we see a fusion of masculine and feminine as we integrate quantitative and qualitative aspects of learning.

What follows here is a list of questions that you can ask, depending on which creative journey you're on, to help you evaluate after every spiral.

Questions to Ask During Introspection Phases of Progress Spirals

For product development, ask yourself:

- What did I accomplish?

- What am I celebrating?

- What went really well?

- What's the best feedback that I got?

- How did my users engage with the product or the material?

- What didn't go so well?

- What lessons did I learn?

- What was the worst piece of feedback I received?

- Should I release the worst piece of feedback I got or should I incorporate it into the next version?

- What was the best constructive criticism I received that I definitely want to integrate?

- Am I connecting the way I wanted to connect?

- Am I on the right path with this project?

- Is there anything about the project path that needs to change?

- If I'm still heading in the right direction, what's the next logical step?

- Is the next logical step the one I'd planned or should I be doing something different?

For business development, here are some questions you can ask in the Introspection phase:

- What are we celebrating?

- What successes have there been?

- What milestones have we achieved?

- Who needs to be acknowledged?

- What isn't going so well?

- What lessons have we learned?

- Are we reaching the right market?

- Is our key messaging in line with what we're offering, what our values are, and who our clients are?

- Are there any new, emerging markets we should be focusing on?

- If we're focusing on the same markets, are there any new offerings we need to be making to serve those markets effectively?

- What needs to change about the logistics and infrastructure of the way we do business?

- How is the team doing?

- Are the employees and subcontractors happy and thriving?

- What kind of support do the employees and subcontractors need to do their job really well?

- What kind of support do I need as a leader to do my job really well?

- How do we move forward from here?

- Are all the physical and logistical aspects of the business (the website, the office, and the marketing collateral) in place and still effective?

- How do I want to be engaging with my clients and meeting them where they are?

- What does my outreach look like?

- Do I need to change my strategy around outreach?

- Do I need to change my strategy around sales?

- How is my pipeline doing?

- Do I need to make any adjustments as to how I move potential clients through the pipeline and create customers?

Finally, **for personal development**, here are some questions you can ask yourself when it's time to evaluate:

- What am I celebrating?

- What have my successes been?

- What's not going well?

- What lessons have I learned?

- What am I grateful for?

- What do I need to release physically or let go of?

- What do I need more of in my life to support myself physically?

- What do I need to release or let go of to be thriving intellectually?

- What do I need to add into my life to be thriving intellectually?

- What do I need to release or let go of to be pursuing my passions and my life's purpose?

- What do I need add into my life to pursue my passions and my life's purpose?

- What do I need to release or let go of to be thriving spiritually and emotionally?

- What do I need to invite into my life to be thriving spiritually and emotionally?

This is a good time to consider whether all of your needs—physical, intellectual, and spiritual, as well as needs related to your passion and purpose—have changed. Don't assume that because you were a runner in high school that running is always going to be your exercise of choice. Your body may need different things at different times in your life. Don't assume that you know the answers without giving it some thought. The Introspection phase is a good time to go really deep and explore any new needs you might have.

These questions are not an exhaustive list by any means. Ask yourself the questions that are going to move you forward. But above all, don't be afraid to dive deep. Don't be afraid to question everything. Don't be afraid to make drastic changes or go back to the drawing board.

Always remember that Introspection is not wasted time. It is stillness, because it is savasana. It is quiet and it's dark. But it isn't wasted time. We must have to remember that the Introspection phase is about germination and preparation. There can't be any moving forward, any advancement of the creative process, without this pause.

CHAPTER TEN

Inspiration

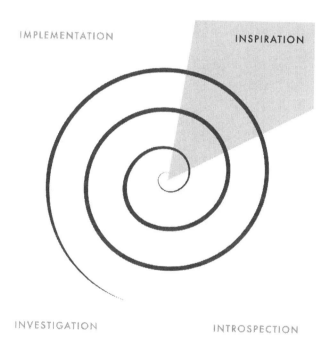

IMPLEMENTATION

INSPIRATION

INVESTIGATION

INTROSPECTION

HOW DOES THE SEED ACTUALLY TRANSFORM INTO A PLANT? There's magic to it. We don't fully understand how it happens exactly. We don't completely understand the mechanics of germination. It's that magical step of inception, of fertilization, of germination, of sprouting. It's transformation.

All of that mystery and magic is in the energy of Inspiration. This is where the true creative work happens. You are going to come up with a solution—whether that's on a personal level, on a business level, or on a product level—that has never been conceived of before. This is where disruptive innovation happens.

The questions that you asked yourself in the Introspection phase form the scaffolding that creates this beautiful, open space in which magic can happen. Without that solid, supportive structure, you don't have the space for Inspiration.

In the Introspection phase, your questions were focused on what happened in the recent past and what things are like in this present moment. The big questions that dominate the Inspiration phase are:

- What do I want to do next?

- What am I solving next?

- Why is this solution important?

- How can I address the questions from the Intro-spection phase in a creative way, in a way that's fun and playful? How can I make it light, joyful, easy, new, and fresh?

Inspiration is where you let the ideas flow. You brainstorm. And in brainstorming, you conceive something new, something that has never existed before. Instead of using linear thinking and connecting the same old dots, you can use web-like, trans-contextual thinking, connecting seemingly disparate subjects or items and putting them together in new ways.

This is an introverted phase, so a lot of this is done on paper, in your brain, and in your heart. There's a lot of internal excitement, because you are riding the emotional wave of inspiration. You feel the strength of the passion about what you can do. You get a glimpse of the future here. Possibilities are endless, and you're playing in unlimited potential.

This phase of the spiral is also dominated by feminine energy. Creativity and innovation are connected to the ultimate creation of new life, which is part of the feminine aspect. And it's a phase of potential energy: stillness combined with a great view of all the possibilities at your fingertips.

The Engineering Process

In the engineering process, the Inspiration phase is about possibility. *Innovation* is a word that we often identify with engineering and technology, even though it's applicable in many domains. This is the fun part, the part where you get to be disruptive (you little rebel, you). This is the part where you're going where no one has gone before, and you're solving new problems in new ways. This is where engineers become inventors of the future. In the engineering process, after you've established either what the vision is or how the vision has changed, the Inspiration phase is where you're actually solving the problem or achieving the goal you set out to pursue.

Since there's a lot of brainstorming and idea generation that's happening here, you're going to have to evaluate the ideas so that you can select which one(s) to pursue. Idea evaluation and selection is a critical piece of this phase. In the midst of your flow of brilliant ideas, you must pluck one out and say, "Yes, this is the one." It's not that you can never implement the other ideas, but you're making a strategic decision to focus on one and see where it takes you, knowing that you may well come back around to the others in subsequent spirals. But you might not.

In engineering, there might be trade studies to help with this evaluation and selection of ideas. Trade studies typically involve gathering some data to help make this selection, so this selection could actually be a spiral in and of itself. The next time around the spiral, you might take that one choice and get inspired about the deeper details. How exactly does it get implemented in a creative way? How is it going to solve the unique problems of this situation? Does the solution have Vitruvius's three key features of a good architecture: utility, sustainability, and beauty?

Seasonal Archetype: Spring

The Inspiration phase is connected with spring, and spring is a time when things come back to life. It's that time of germination, of sprouting, of exploding out of the closed, dark world that was the seed. It's the beginning of stepping out into the light, but it's still full of potential. Buds start to form, but you don't know how the flowers or leaves are going to thrive. If you're a bear that's been hibernating, it's time to start waking up, stretching out, finding something to eat, and getting ready to take those first steps into action.

We're still focused on *being* instead of *doing*, and we're still solidly rooted in the potential, in the possibility. But here are the stirrings of activity. We're starting to create the forward motion that's going to lead us into the *doing* part of the cycle—the part that's going to convert our potential energy into kinetic energy.

These innovations are necessarily going to reflect your inner *being*: your values, passions, skills, and superpowers. That's why you can bring something truly unique into the world. It's a reflection of your core being. Not what you do but who you are.

Elemental Archetype: Air

Spring is often associated with the element of Air, which relates to spirituality, intellect, and higher thinking. Even if you're doing something extremely practical—producing a product, building a business or an organization—that connection to spirituality is so important, and it comes to us in this phase in the form of inspiration itself.

Dr. Wayne Dyer described inspiration as being rooted in the phrase "in the spirit" or "inhabited by spirit." The act of being inspired, of ideating, of innovating, of being disruptive, of creating something where nothing has been created before, is a spiritual experience. We would do well to remember—even as we work in more traditional environments that may carry more masculine-dominated energy—that inspiration, this influx of spirit, is part of the natural cycle, and it's what enables innovation.

There is no innovation without inspiration. While you can't control inspiration, you can set up the conditions for it. The preparation that we did in the Introspection phase sets up the structure that's required to create the conditions for Inspiration to happen. No one knows exactly how a seed germinates and begins to sprout. But if you create the right conditions—by putting the seed in the ground, in the dark, in nutritive soil, and giving it water—most of the time, your seed will germinate and sprout. Once you've created the right conditions, you just have to allow it to happen.

And so it is with Inspiration. We create the environment. We let the ideas come, and we welcome them. We allow ourselves to look at things from new angles, new perspectives. We allow ourselves to put things together that haven't been put together before. We become, then, disruptively innovative, and it all comes from simply allowing it to happen. Which is directly connected to the Air element and to spring.

Inspiration is also about higher thinking. Instead of thinking about the way things always were, it's about taking on the bigger perspective on how they could be. Birds are associated with the Air element. Think of eagles, falcons, and hawks. They're traveling on the currents of the air, elemental Air, and they have the big-picture view.

They can see the entire landscape laid out before them. We don't call it a bird's-eye view for nothing!

How Do You Know You're in the Inspiration Phase?

The Inspiration phase is pretty fun, to be quite honest. You stay up at night because the ideas just keep coming. You probably want to keep a notebook with you wherever you go because you'll find yourself struck by a whole bunch of new ideas. It might feel distracting, but you're not being scatterbrained. It's just the Inspiration phase of the spiral. You might be dreaming big right now, and because the grass is always greener on the other side of the spiral, maybe you wish you were *doing* more and dreaming less.

There's a time and a place for dreaming, and now is that time. If you're dreaming and seeing potential everywhere, that's a great indication that you're in the Inspiration phase and ready to let it flow! It's time to innovate, to think outside the box, to run down rabbit trails. Allow Inspiration to come in and fill you up, because you can never force it. When it's flowing, you've got to use it.

It can be frustrating, though, to be in the shadow side of this phase. *Innovation* means change, and change can be scary. Another word that gets kicked around in this type of phase is *transformation*. It's transformation of the way you think, transformation of how you do things, transformation of what the status quo looks like. You're like a caterpillar crawling into the chrysalis and then reemerging as a butterfly. Transformation can look and feel like total destruction when you're in the middle of it.

It sounds really great to say, "Oh yeah, I'm feeling so inspired! I can see possibility and potential!" But don't be alarmed if you also experience the upheaval of everything changing. If that feels unstable to you, like being crushed under the weight of your own possibility, know that it's a normal part of the Inspiration phase. It's another indicator that you're here. And if you know that you're in it, you can leverage the gifts of Inspiration instead of freaking out about change and scatter.

How Do You Leverage the Energy and Gifts of Inspiration?

First of all, make sure that you allow Inspiration to happen. Open yourself to it. You're going to have a lot of ideas, so don't fight that. Let them flow.

Make sure you have a way to document all your ideas. You could carry a notebook with you. You could use a note app or a voice-recording app on your phone. You could keep a text file open on your computer. Whatever solution makes sense for you, make sure you can document the ideas so you don't lose them. Try to turn off your inner critic, who immediately jumps to what the Implementation is going to look like and tries to tell you why it's not going to work. You can process the ideas later, in a different spiral phase. Right now, no idea is a bad idea.

When you're in the initial Discovery Spiral, you're going to be looking ahead at the very first steps to take. You're inspired by the big picture and may want to accomplish everything all at once. That can feel overwhelming. Remember that Rome wasn't built in a day. This is an iterative process, and you'll have lots of spirals in which to explore and develop all your ideas. So, if you're inspired in the Discovery Spiral with lots of ideas from all aspects of your big-picture vision, let them flow! Write down whatever comes, and tell the voice that's shouting, "It's too big!" that you realize you don't have to build it all at once.

The other way you can approach the Discovery Spiral is to start small. Think about baby steps. You may feel that you don't currently have the capability to build the final output that's in your head. You may not have any clue how to get there from here. That's totally okay! Use this first spiral to do a deep dive into the problem you're trying to solve. How can you observe, listen to, and relate to the client, to your team, to yourself? How can you bring disparate things together in innovative ways? Write down your insights. What can you do right now, from right where you are?

For Progress Spirals, part of the Inspiration phase is choosing the scope for your current spiral. What are you getting inspired to *do* in the coming phases? Are you getting inspired on the level of the big-picture vision and then working down into details in subsequent iterations? Or are you getting inspired to start with something small and increase your scope incrementally? The spiral can work in either direction—broad to detailed or detailed to broad. To some extent, it depends on what you're working on.

For product development, I recommend starting with something that you can do on a small scale right now. Start with a small scope, a custom solution, a smaller audience, and highly specific cases, and use those to learn. Then as you spiral around, you can expand and get successively bigger, broader, more standardized, more automated, and more generalized.

For business development, you might start at a broader level. You might say, "Well, generally, I'm trying to help people recover from trauma and addiction," and you'll spiral initially on that big topic. In the process of working on that during the first spiral, you'll get inspired around specific things you can do, ways you want to work, and people you want to help. When you come back around into your next Inspiration phase, you can get a little more focused. At that point, you might say, "Okay, what exactly does that look like, helping people get through trauma? I want to help get people through trauma and addiction using yoga." Then, you'll get a little bit more specific. When things are specific and focused, it's easier to take action.

For personal development, you could start either way—broadly with big ideas or focused with simple ideas. To some extent, it will depend on your personality and how you prefer to begin.

Whichever way you begin, it does help to be deliberate about choosing the scope and to set the initial parameters around how you're going to move forward. Again, you want to create conditions that are favorable for Inspiration to happen. You want to invite it in. Once you're inspired, it's easy to take action and create momentum at whatever level you're working, and momentum is what really makes this effort sustainable.

To leverage the Inspiration phase, let the ideas flow. Set a scope that creates the right environment for ideation and innovation. Don't be afraid to put weird stuff together, to think outside the box, or to do things differently from the way they've ever been done. Feel the joy of the fresh air in your face. There's not a whole lot more to it than that. Enjoy it and let it flow. Open yourself to Inspiration. And when you're ready, it's time to implement.

CHAPTER ELEVEN

Implementation

IN THIS SPIRAL PHASE, WE'RE GOING TO take the ideas and Inspiration from the previous phase and actually do something about them. Some people think that innovation happens when you're actually building something. In reality, the innovation has already been done, and the Inspiration has already been harnessed. The dominant question for this phase of the spiral is "how?" How are you going to make your brilliant ideas real?

There's a lot of detail in this phase. There's a lot of trying things, making them work, putting them together. You can start to see all your ideas coming together into a cohesive *thing*.

This is where the work gets done. It's time now to bring this thing into being, to follow through, and to build it. It's time to dig in and get 'er done. I'm not saying this because it's always hard—it's not. Sometimes it can be a grind, and sometimes it's easy and obvious how everything should click together. It might be boring, or it might come with lots of joy. But any way you slice it, it's a totally different feeling from the Inspiration phase.

The beauty is that the Inspiration phase should jumpstart your momentum for the Implementation phase. Inspiration lights that emotional fire of excitement within you that can then carry you into and through this time of *doing*.

We've swung now firmly into the *doing* part of the cycle. It's no longer about *being*. It's no longer about *potential* energy. It's now about *kinetic* energy, motion, and momentum.

If you're a seed, you sprouted into the potential of becoming in the Inspiration phase. The Implementation phase is all about blooming, coming fully into the manifestation of those ideas that were always latent under the surface, ready to break through. The bloom is unfurling during this phase into the expression of its beauty and potential.

The Engineering Process

In terms of the engineering process, the Implementation phase is about building. It's about getting your hands on the hardware, writing the lines of code, or getting words onto the paper. It's a manifestation of all of these ideas that have been built up in the previous two phases. They're coming into reality now.

This manifestation looks different depending on where you are in the project cycle. If you're in the beginning spirals of a project, this could be a model. Models can exist as descriptions or sketches on paper, software models, or small-scale physical models. In the middle of project development, it could be a prototype. It could be a module of hardware that's a small part of the whole thing. Toward the end of the project, you might be building flight hardware—the whole, full-on, integrated spacecraft that's ready to be launched.

All of those examples of manifestations of an idea fall into this Implementation phase in the spiral. During each progressive spiral, the Implementation builds on the ideas and learning from the previous one to evolve into something more mature and closer to being the real thing, ready for deployment.

Perhaps you do one spiral to get to a model. In that initial spiral, you go through the Introspection and Inspiration phases to get to the model Implementation. It's only after the model exists and you've been able to take it through the Investigation phase, evaluate it (during the Introspection phase), and get inspired about how to move it forward that you can come back around in the second spiral and implement a prototype. And guess what? Building the prototype happens in this Implementation phase too. In each spiral, you refine what you've got so that you can eventually build production-quality, flight-ready hardware.

Seasonal Archetype: Summer

The seasonal archetype for the Implementation phase is summer.

You know the feeling of summer. It's time to be free. Plants rise up out of the earth and bloom. The trees leaf out. Things are green and lush and abundant. You can do a lot of living outside when it's warm.

This energy is definitely moving out into extraversion. You're building things that can start to become visible to the outside world. You don't mind that you're becoming visible. You start to create a buzz around what you're doing so that eventually you'll be able to sell it or to attract fellow members of your tribe. There's an allure and a charisma, the way a flower bloom attracts a bee, when you start to manifest your ideas and build them into reality.

Elemental Archetype: Fire

Speaking of being hot and attractive, the elemental archetype for the Implementation phase is Fire. Fire is the transformational element. We're working the alchemy of transforming ideas and thoughts into physical reality, into deliberate actions that create the life we love, or into a business that is actually profitable. Fire is that alchemical element that provides the chemical reaction that transforms matter, just as we transform thought into reality.

The shadow side of the Fire element is that it can get out of hand. It can consume. In Implementation we throw ourselves into the *doing* with fervor... But when does it become too much? *Can* it become too much? When does it start to consume us?

I'm not here to give you the answer to those questions, or to pretend to know where the line is. It's something to be aware of though, since this action mode is more of a masculine energy. Our culture glorifies the untempered masculine, often to the point of toxicity: workaholism to the point of burnout and achievement at all costs. We don't want to be consumed by our own Fire. How will we implement the amazing vision that we crafted if we burn ourselves up in the process?

How Do You Know You're Ready for the Implementation Phase?

You're probably ready for the Implementations phase if:

- You're motivated to sit down and make things happen

- You've had enough talk and you're ready to take action

- You're ready to put your hands on something that previously existed only in your brain

- You're ready to dive in with both feet

Ride that wave and make it happen!

It's possible to be frustrated with the level of focus required for the Implementation phase because you may feel as though you have tunnel vision. You're only focusing on doing this one thing in order to make it happen, and it's all you can think about. Somewhere at the back of your mind there might be a panicky voice that says, "You're neglecting everything else!" But there isn't anything fundamentally wrong here.

Right now, focus is what you need. Recognize that you're in the Implementation phase and embrace the focus. Don't worry so much about the big picture because you know you're going to come back around the spiral again. Trust the spiral and that you'll see the big picture again soon enough. Right now, it's okay to be in the details. It's okay to be down in the weeds.

How Do You Leverage the Energy and Gifts of the Implementation Phase?

Working all the details is a really great thing to do right now. Focus on your one idea and run it to ground. Make lists. Call in help. Write down everything you know you need and the places where you see gaps. If you feel good about it, you could give yourself a deadline, or maybe you'll have a deadline imposed upon you by external forces. Make yourself a schedule or a work plan and then build, build, build.

You don't need to make room for innovation now. You don't need to stop and think too hard about what's going on. You've made a plan, and now it's time to execute it. This is the time to ante up. Hold yourself accountable for showing up to do the work.

There's a time in the spiral (hint: it was the previous two phases) for you to sit back and allow things to come to you. This is not that time.

This is active time. Harness it and go for it! You might push a little harder than you normally do. You might feel as if you're out of balance on the side of *doing* and not really *being*. There's nothing that's wrong with that. Go ahead and leverage it! Make your lists, make your project plans, and then go, go, go. That's how you leverage the Implementation phase.

Coming out of this phase, you'll want to see something really concrete.

For product development, you'll want to mock up your prototype. Or perhaps you've got the next version of your product ready to go.

At the end of the Implementation phase, you'll have something that's ready to offer to a client, with all of the details in place that are appropriate for the scope you chose in Inspiration. You're going to have the flow completely mapped out.

For business development, this is where you are putting things into place and making changes. You might have to purchase some resources. You might have to implement a marketing strategy. This is where you go and *do* it. You actually create your marketing collateral and then put it out there. You start to get visible. My father-in-law (a machinist and entrepreneur himself) would say that you are "hanging out your shingle." What do you need to put yourself out there to the world as a business owner? What do you need to explain your value proposition? These are the nitty-gritty details of having a business and turning what you have to offer into cash.

If your work is within an organization, this could be where you implement a new initiative. Now is when you gather your people around you and say, "This is how we're going to do it. This is how we're going to make us better. This is how I want to lead from now on." Maybe that's creating a new type of meeting rhythm. Maybe it's a new way of engaging with people at a meeting so that they stay involved and excited. *How* is the dominant question. Take all of that momentum, apply it to the plan you made, and go make it a reality.

For personal development, it's time to execute your plan. Try something new. Heck, try something old! "Move confidently in the direction of your dreams and live the life you have imagined," as Henry David Thoreau said. He'll tell you that you're about to "meet with success unexpected in common hours."

Are you getting the idea here? Are you catching my drift? Can you feel the energy? Are you pumped?

Shift into *doing* and create the thing you want to see in the world.

CHAPTER TWELVE

Investigation

IMPLEMENTATION

INSPIRATION

INVESTIGATION

INTROSPECTION

I RECENTLY TOOK UP A TAE KWON DO PRACTICE. In each martial arts class, I participate and practice with a dozen other students of various ranks. There's no way to hide from either the instructor or my classmates. Not that I would want to hide—getting feedback, suggestions, and critique from my classmates is a valuable part of the experience. But it feels vulnerable and I can't say it's completely comfortable. Still, I embrace it as a necessary part of my cycle of growth. Periodically, I will have to undergo formal testing in order to advance in rank to higher belts. These formal tests definitely represent the Investigation phase of the spiral well—they are literally a gateway to a whole new level of tae kwon do practice. Belt testing—Investigation, if you will—prepares me to kick off a brand-new, leveled-up spiral.

Investigation is the final phase of the spiral before you come around again into Introspection. You may have started to get visible in Implementation, but in the Investigation phase, it's time to really put it out there and engage the world. The energy here is quite extraverted. It's still action-oriented, focused on *doing*, but there's an element of listening for feedback as well. During Investigation, you aren't just putting your work out there blindly. You're looking (and asking!) for a response, perhaps collecting data to gauge how it's going. The ultimate objective of Investigation is to understand if what you're pouring your soul into is effective or not. It needs to be effective for you, the creator, and it needs to be effective for the recipient. With data in play, it can get pretty quantitative in this phase, and that, along with words like *analysis* and *tracking* might have you recoiling in horror. Luckily, this all flows neatly out of the work you've already done, and as we've demonstrated, being in flow with the spiral phases brings a certain sense of ease.

The energy of Investigation is analytical, extraverted, and relational. We're still in this *do*-oriented, deliberate action-taking, and rational-analytical side of the spiral—in other words, the masculine side of the spiral. However, even though we're in masculine energy here, it's a more passive form of it. Implementation is an active masculine phase in which you're *doing* a lot and building something out of nothing, calling it into reality. It sounds like a contradiction in terms, but Investigation is a passive form of *doing*. You're putting whatever you're creating out there and then accepting the results and being open to receiving feedback. The beginnings of receptivity are preparing you to cycle back to Introspection in the next phase.

The Engineering Process

Investigation is associated with the Testing phase in engineering. So, once you've built something, you've got to make sure that the thing does what you think it's going to do and that it performs the way you think it's going to perform. If you're building a spacecraft, for example, you might put hardware through environmental tests, thermal tests, and vibrational tests, to make sure that it withstands the environment it needs to withstand.

You also might do path testing, meaning that you're going to try every single variation how your solution will be used. Then, you have to test every use single case. It's rigorous and thorough.

Seasonal Archetype: Autumn

The seasonal archetype for the Investigation phase is autumn. Autumn carries the energy of harvest time. This is truly reaping the fruits of your labor. What labor, you ask? First, you put all of this intellectual and spiritual energy into ideating and innovating. Then, you put your physical energy into doing the actual creating and Implementation. Now, you've come around the spiral to release your labor into the wild. Now, you're going to see the results.

The harvest can manifest in different ways. Always at the top of the list is how you feel about seeing your work released into the world. The traditional definition of "results" is seeing your work make a difference and solve the problem you set out to solve. Even if you are in an early spiral, and the output of Implementation is not a full-blown solution, the objective of Investigation is to show progress towards that fully fleshed idea.

Another form of the harvest in investigation is the feedback you get from the work you've done in this spiral. You don't want to miss any of the choicest, ripest insights that will tell you what you need to know about how to move forward and will guide you into the next spiral. You may want to spend some time thinking about what kind of data you need to collect, what kind of fruits you need to harvest. Make sure you harvest thoroughly in order to get what you need to evaluate and move forward with confidence.

Elemental Archetype: Water

Water is the elemental archetype traditionally associated with autumn and is now associated with Investigation. Water is the element of emotion. You might say, "How does Investigation connect to emotion?" Investigation is about connecting with people. It's about seeing how they interact with your ideas, your Implementation, your vision. Ultimately, no matter which creative path you're on, decisions aren't made based on cold, hard facts. The facts can help, but decisions are ultimately made based on emotion. Why? Because we're humans, and that's how we roll as a species.

For product or business development, your customers need to connect with your product or business on an emotional level. I've worked in several different industries, some of which you might think have no connection to the emotional realm at all. It doesn't matter which industry I've been in, whether it's flying spacecraft, commissioning energy systems, or coaching spiritual teachers. All of my clients make emotional decisions. They need to connect with the solution in an emotional way. They need to be excited about it. They need to feel comfortable and secure in it.

The Investigation phase is so emotionally connected that a lot of the data you're going to bring back from your experimentation is about how it feels. How did the client feel before and after? How did I feel before and after?

For personal development, Investigation holds the same connection to emotion, only it's more individually focused on you. How did these changes that you've made make you feel? How do they make your family feel? What's the vibe? What's the vibe you're creating for yourself and for your tribe?

That's why putting things out where they're visible, where they can be tested and witnessed by actual people is so deeply connected to the emotional energy of Water. It's sort of funny because here we are in a masculine energy phase of *doing* with methodical, directed action and logical, rational analysis. But we're also in the flow of Water and emotion. It's good to remember that even as we're being methodical and rigorous, there's still a certain amount of flow present.

The spiral isn't meant to reinforce the separation inherent in these dichotomies. It integrates them. So, even as we are rigorous, data driven and analytical, we are still flowing and we are still emotionally connected.

How Do you Know You're in the Investigation Phase?

The key quality of this phase is your connection to the outside world. If you're putting your work in front of people, allowing yourself to be visible and receive feedback, you're in the Investigation phase. If you're co-creating with others, if you are engaging in community for the benefit of yourself and of that community, you're in Investigation.

You may feel more extraverted than usual. As in Implementation, because you're so focused on this particular solution, you may again feel that you've lost your sense of the big picture.

You're going to learn one of two things in this phase. You may learn that you're on the right path and that you need to keep going forward. That's exciting because you're probably going to celebrate a success. But you might also learn that this is not the right direction, and you might want to make some changes. That can be super frustrating.

Investigation is a vulnerable phase. If you're feeling exposed, especially to judgment, feedback, or criticism, you're in the Investigation phase. You may also be receiving praise, accolades, and celebrations. Feedback, whether complimentary or critical, can be wonderful, but it can be draining at the same time. Obviously, it's more draining for someone who tends to function as an introvert to be visible for a sustained amount of time than it is for an extravert. Regardless, it can be simultaneously exciting and terrifying, no matter who you are.

You're going to face down some of those fears and inner demons in this phase. If you're feeling those prickles of the fear of being seen, that's probably because you're either about to move into Investigation or you're already there. It's a good time to at least acknowledge that some fears are there. Acknowledgment paves the way to handling those fears or moving around them. Tell fear to take a seat, because it's time. It's time to roll out.

It doesn't matter if you're presenting in front of one person or an arena of 10,000. It means you're in Investigation.

How Do You Leverage the Energy and Gifts of Investigation?

For product or business development, it's time to get in front of people deliberately. The right people. Your desired clients.

For personal development, you're going to be visible as you take action, and you're going to be bringing what you do out into your community. This concept is certainly illustrated by my experience with tae kwon do. Not all personal pursuits are quite so public, but the spirit of the Investigation is the same—be bold, test yourself, test your practice, be visible, level up.

The whole creative spiral is for naught if the work isn't eventually out in the world. You've heard the phrase "Don't create in a vacuum." Investigation is how you avoid creating in a vacuum. You start where you are, you come up with an innovative solution, you implement it to the level that you can implement it, and you trust that you're going to learn what you need to learn to prove the concept or change direction.

Be very deliberate about the data that you want to take. Sure, you're going to do your evaluation in the Introspection phase, but don't wait until that phase to ask the right questions. You need to get feedback on what you're doing. The wheels are turning, the ribbon has been cut, and your work is going to make a difference. Go into that situation thinking about these questions: "What data do I need to let me know that I'm being successful?" "What data will I need to help me improve this in the future?" You could answer these questions with quantitative or qualitative data—it really depends on what you're working on. Trust that you will know what kind of data you need.

Remember to connect emotionally—to yourself, to your team, to your clients. Emotional connection is what makes us all human. It's the ultimate common ground. While you are taking data, ask questions. How do other people feel about my work? How do I feel about my work?

Emotional connection is the key to leveraging the Investigation phase—to turning it around into newer, better solutions, and to turning it into powerful, focused marketing material. You'll grow forward through your next spirals only if you are emotionally connected within the process.

Once you have put your work into the world and you have started to reap the harvest of results, it's time to circle back to Introspection and take some time to integrate what you have learned.

CHAPTER THIRTEEN

Deployment (Bonus Phase)

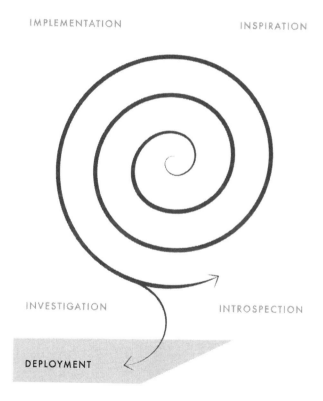

I WOULD BE REMISS IF I DIDN'T MENTION the bonus phase of the spiral. Deployment isn't one of the iterative spiral steps, but it is a critical piece of building a business and curating a suite of products, services, and solutions that drive revenue without intensive creative input from you.

This goes back to the Microsoft example we discussed earlier. After each iteration of the Windows operating system, Microsoft deploys a new version to become a revenue-generating machine, even as the development team begins work on the next version.

You can use this exact model to start driving revenue with your product before it's "ready"—before it's in the format of the final vision.

Remember the adage that you only have to be a step or two in front of your clients to lead them? That's where this deployment phase really comes in handy—you can offer your expertise while you are still learning.

Although the Deployment phase feels most useful in the business setting, it can be used in personal development too. You could decide to introduce your kids to your chosen pursuit before you're officially at expert status and learn together. You could implement a partial solution for home organization that, while imperfect, really helps you feel like you're making progress.

Think of the Deployment phase as one of the intermediate steps that mark your progress. Deployment milestones can make the spiral look rather linear after all, but don't be fooled—the iterations are still there underneath, supporting each stepwise milestone along the way.

CHAPTER FOURTEEN

Dividing the Spiral

HUMANS ARE NOT MEANT TO BE STATIC, or worse, stagnant. Humans are meant to be in motion. We fluctuate. We are messy and organic, and we're on a constant trajectory of growth. But though growth can feel messy and in continuous flux, we aren't unpredictable. There's a predictable rhythm, pattern, and structure that underlie everything we do. And that's where the spiral comes in—the gentle, predictable rhythm that guides our seasons of growth as the seasons set the rhythm of the Earth.

IMPLEMENTATION
SUMMER

INSPIRATION
SPRING

AUTUMN
INVESTIGATION

WINTER
INTROSPECTION

Spiral and the Seasons

If you divide this seasonal creative spiral by drawing a vertical line that bisects it so that you have summer and autumn on one side of the line and winter and spring on the other side of the line, you'll have a pretty good division between masculine aspects on the summer/autumn side and feminine aspects on the winter/spring side. You could also replace masculine/feminine with yang/yin, if you prefer—it's the same idea.

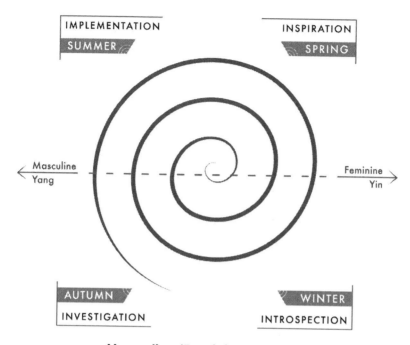

Masculine/Feminine Aspects

I want to pause here and carefully remind you that this has absolutely nothing to do with gender. It has absolutely nothing to do with whether you identify as male or female, or something else entirely. It's simply a representation of qualities that are existent in all humans.

You may be tempted to think that dividing the spiral into masculine and feminine sides gives you the excuse to say, "Well, I'm a man. I'm incapable of rest, retreat, or innovative thinking." We know that's simply not true. Or that it gives you the opportunity to say, "Well, I'm a woman, so I'm incapable of taking action, executing a structured plan, and gathering feedback and data." That's definitely not true either. I mean, if I were to make those statements about myself, you'd tell me I'm being ridiculous.

So, let's not fool ourselves into thinking that because we write *masculine* and *feminine* on either side of the spiral, we're exempt from going through those spiral phases. It's simply an opportunity for you to access and use your innate masculine or feminine aspects. You can let them come out, let them play, give them exercise, or you can let them breathe and rest for a while.

Returning to the divided spiral, you could put *outward-facing* or *extraversion* with the masculine. Then, you could put *inward-turning, inward-facing,* or *introversion* alongside the feminine.

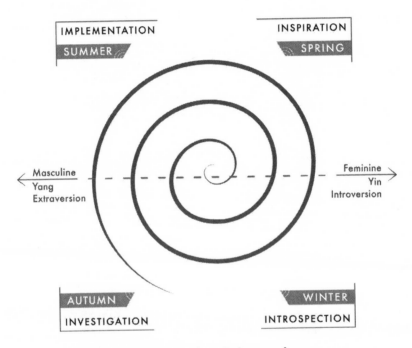

IMPLEMENTATION

SUMMER

INSPIRATION

SPRING

← Masculine
Yang
Extraversion

Feminine →
Yin
Introversion

AUTUMN

INVESTIGATION

WINTER

INTROSPECTION

Extraversion/Introversion

Again, I don't want to hear you say, "I'm this, not that." If you're an extravert, you still need the inward-turning time in your creative cycle. Perhaps those times are shorter for you, or perhaps they require extra effort for you to leverage the energies of those spiral phases. And similarly, if you're an introvert, that doesn't mean you're never in front of people, never visible, or never putting your ideas out into the world. It just means that maybe that time is shorter, more focused, more potent, more concentrated, and that the majority of your time is spent in the other portions of the spiral. Maybe it means you have to put a little more energy and focus into those parts of the spiral that don't come quite so naturally to you.

In the "extraverted" part of the spiral, you have a tendency to be more outward-facing than inward-facing and more extraverted than introverted, and we see the dance swing in that direction. As you come around the spiral, you'll swing and shift and dance back over to the "introverted" side, even if that's not your preferred way of operating. Even if your style of introversion looks completely different from someone else's, you still have it.

Some more aspects to add to the spiral: *doing*, an action focus, on the left. And *being*, a receptive focus, on the right. *Analysis* goes left, and *intuition* goes right. You could add *left-brained*, which, funny enough, goes on the left (see what I did there?); *right-brained* would then go on the right.

On the left side you have more structure. Even though there are structural elements on the right side, the left side is all about structure. It's about executing on a process. It's about gathering data in a rigorous fashion. For Implementation/Investigation, you have structured features such as getting the logistics in order, executing a process, or collecting data. For Introspection/Inspiration, what do you have? You have flow. The work is more open ended and less rigid.

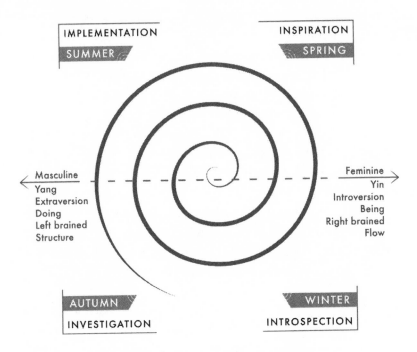

Structure and Flow Aspects

Guy Kawasaki, former chief evangelist at Apple, famously said, "What really matters happens at the edges." This is one of my favorite quotes of all time. The line that we drew across the spiral forms an edge between spring and summer, between Air and Fire, between the influx of Inspiration and the transformation that occurs when the Inspiration gets Implemented.

To me, there's a very natural transition over that line. It's easy to make the transition from "Oh my gosh, I have this great idea," into "Now let's build the idea," because you've started to build emotional momentum, and the momentum carries you over the line.

Similarly, I think there's a potentially easy transition from Investigation into Introspection (aka fall to winter, or Water to Earth) because you've collected the data, so now you'll naturally want to take a look at that data and learn from it. There's a natural urge to want to take what you've learned, go sit with it, and figure out what it means to you. That's not to say that being in the resting part is always easy. I think of all of the phases of the spiral, the winter phase, Introspection, is often the most difficult in our *do*-oriented society.

Now let's draw another line perpendicular to the first line. The first line represents primary dichotomies that set off the spiral phases. But there aren't two phases, there are four. There are some secondary traits that link Inspiration/Implementation and Investigation/Introspection. The former are active phases, whereas the latter are passive phases.

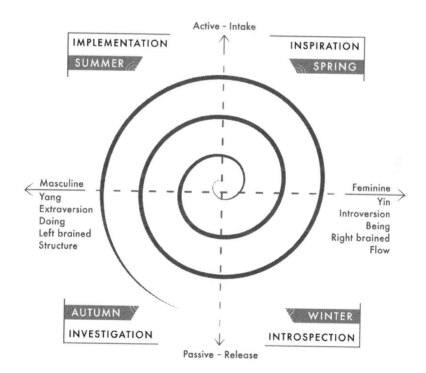

Passive/Active Aspects

Introspection, for example, is a passive form of feminine energy, all about rest and reflection, stillness and receptivity. Even though you're still in that receptive mode when you move into Inspiration, it's a much more active time. You claim that influx of Inspiration and make it your own. You start to draw the possibility of manifestation down from the ether and dare to begin to put some legs under your dreams. The act of creation, right up to creating life itself, is a very active, yet still feminine, quality.

Similarly, on the other side of the spiral, when you're in the Implementation phase, bringing an idea into reality, you're building something. That's an active masculine energy. The tools are in your hands, whether those are your actual, physical hands or your metaphorical, intellectual hands. And you're constructing the idea in a methodical, structured way so that your idea isn't only being realized, but it's robust as well. But then, the Investigation phase—though it's still structured, rational, and logical—is more passively masculine. Investigation is highly dependent upon interactions with others: the client or the community. Collaboration and receptivity are usually considered to be feminine traits, and indeed, this phase starts to form the transition back to the feminine. But here, in Investigation, we're still leveraging extraversion, analysis, structure, and rationality, so we can identify it as collaborative—or more passive—masculine.

If the spiral is divided on that same active/passive line, the other dichotomy you can put in there is that of intake and release. Inhaling and exhaling is an example of this.

For the Inspiration and Implementation phases, you're inviting in new ideas and new solutions. You're adding to your repertoire or to your product suite. You're expanding.

For the Investigation and Introspection phases you're releasing ideas and solutions. In the Investigation phase, you are releasing your latest idea into the wild to see how it does. You have prepared it and built it up, and now it's time to let it go. In the Introspection phase, the release process is deeper and more personal. What is no longer serving you or no longer aligned with your vision needs to go. You are clearing space and cleansing. You are contracting.

The transitions, the handoffs between all of the phases are graceful, even though the phases all have different (even opposite) energies. It shouldn't feel like shifting without a clutch. It should feel like a dance. It should feel like breathing. It should feel like exhaling and taking that brief pause at emptiness, and then inhaling and taking a brief pause at fullness. It's just that natural.

When we divide the spiral, we take a step back and look at the big-picture view of the spiral movements and transitions, and we can see why these dichotomies emerge.

Potential

Just as the spiral dances between masculine and feminine energies, it also dances between potential and kinetic energy. In physics, potential energy doesn't involve motion. It's a place of stillness, of rest. But it's usually from a high place—a place from which you can take in the sweeping vision of the whole path in front of you before you start plunging downward into action and momentum, picking up hard-to-stop speed. Kinetic energy is inextricably tied to motion. The more motion, the more kinetic energy—but also the less potential as you start to move.

Consider a pendulum.

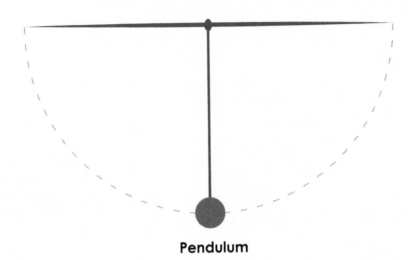

Pendulum

A pendulum is an oscillating, cyclical system, just like the creative spiral, so we can learn some lessons from it. A pendulum is constantly exchanging potential energy for kinetic energy and back again.

In order to talk about kinetic and potential energy, let's take a look at the velocity of the weight at the bottom of the pendulum happily swinging back and forth (we'll call him Bob). Energy, particularly of the kinetic variety, is directly related to velocity (by the equation $\frac{1}{2}mv^2$, if you're feeling nerdy, where m is Bob's mass). Potential energy is related to Bob's height above the ground.

The place where Bob is moving the fastest (most kinetic energy) also happens to occur at the lowest place (least potential energy): the bottom of his swing.

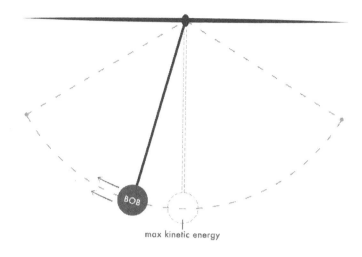

Pendulum—Kinetic Energy

As he swings over to the side, Bob actually comes to rest briefly at the top of his swing, corresponding to the moment of highest potential and lowest kinetic energy. This is key because potential energy isn't only defined by stillness (the lack of kinetic energy) but also by the ability to go somewhere, usually because of being somewhere up high.

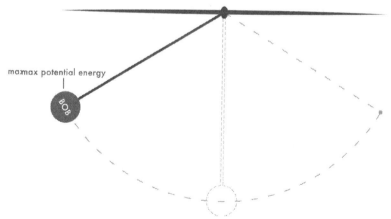

Pendulum—Potential Energy

So, the moment of maximum potential energy occurs at the top of the pendulum swing in that impossible moment of pause at the highest point before swinging down again. The moment of maximum kinetic energy occurs at the bottom of the swing, where all the energy is converted to motion—none of it is stored. If you've ever had the pleasure of playing on a swing (in which case, we'll call *you* Bob), you know that the view is best from the point of extreme height. There's a moment of pause during which you can actually enjoy the view (and it also provides a great launch point for getting off of the swing). On the same pendulum, the moment of maximum kinetic energy occurs at the bottom of the swing, the center point, when you have the highest speed but the most limited view from the lowest point. This spot has its own thrills caused by the motion, or the action.

In the spiral, the Introspection and Inspiration phases are the phases of maximum potential. These are the periods when you're able to pause and take in the view. You are still, but you're also taking the big-picture view of your vision. All possibilities are laid out in front of you, and you can consider what might be.

The Implementation and Investigation phases are kinetic, in motion. These come with their own thrill, not because you have access to all possibilities, but because you've gained momentum along a focused path.

The point is that we are not one thing or the other. We are not this *or* that. We are most certainly this *and* that, although not always all at once. And if we allow these seemingly opposite qualities to fluctuate, flow, and dance, we can focus the energy we would have spent fighting for the attributes on the other side of the spiral on utilizing the gifts of the current phase.

At the highest point of the pendulum's swing, Bob has 100 percent potential energy and 0 percent kinetic energy. When Bob reaches the very bottom of his swing, at the lowest point, it has the maximum velocity. At that moment, it has 100 percent kinetic energy and 0 percent potential energy. These points of the swing are only fractions of a moment, almost impossible to measure, when the pendulum is actually at those moments of extreme potential and extreme kinetic energy. In reality, most of the swing is a blend of the two.

It's the same with the creative spiral. There are so few moments of extreme qualities. As humans, we like to see the dichotomies because extremes are easier to think about. But in reality, the majority of our progress around the spiral is spent in transition, blending a potent cocktail of gifts and skills together in a unique way to serve our creative needs in the present moment.

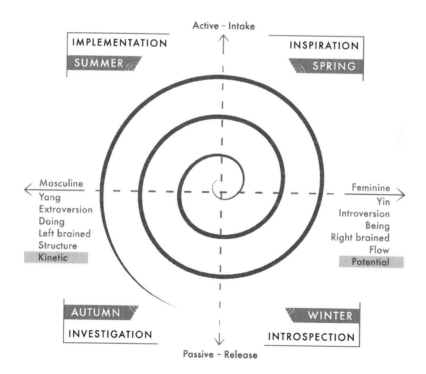

Spiral With Kinetic and Potential Energy Aspects

The dichotomies show up in the spiral, but that doesn't mean that when we flip over from spring into summer, or from Inspiration into Implementation, we've shifted from 100 percent potential to 100 percent kinetic energy. This is a graceful dance. This is surfing the ebb and the flow of the tides. As we transition from Inspiration to Implementation, we're in the surge toward kinetic energy. We're leaving potential behind just for the moment, and it recedes like the tide. We'll come back around to it, in this surging toward kinetic energy, until it's time to fall backward toward potential. It's a continuous flow, a continuous dance.

So, the next time you catch yourself thinking in dichotomy ("I am this, not that"), I want you to remember the spiral. I want you to think about how you're dancing between the two qualities in question. Entertain the idea, just for a moment, that even if you prefer one side of the dichotomy to the other, you might just have all the tools you need to operate on the other side of that dichotomy. Entertain the idea that those tools are powerful for you when used at the right time in your own personal spiral and that they hold the key to unlocking your vision.

CHAPTER FIFTEEN

The Spiral Vortex

A WHILE BACK, THERE WAS A VIDEO that went around on social media that showed the solar system traveling through space. It first showed all of the planets orbiting around our sun. Then the video reminded the viewer that even as we feel as if we're orbiting in circles or ellipses around our sun, the sun is also progressing through physical space, orbiting the center of the Milky Way. As we progress through space, we're not just forming circles around the sun as the Earth travels around it. Our path actually forms a vortex moving forward in space and in time.

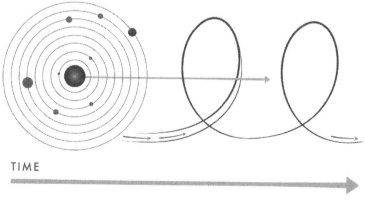

TIME

Solar System Vortex

That's how I like to see this progression of spirals. Sure, we're spiraling all the time. We're going through cycles of rest and action. We're going through cycles of passivity and activity. We are going through cycles of masculine and feminine energies, of structure and flow. But we're not just moving in circles. Because we move forward in growth and knowledge, we move forward as well.

So, the path of growth is not just a spiral. It's a spiral vortex.

TIME

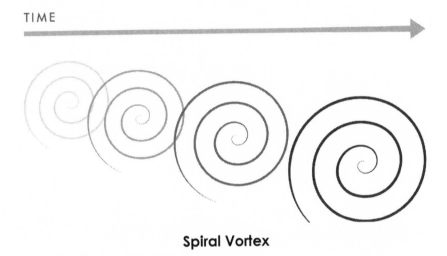

Spiral Vortex

Spiral cycles are inherent in evolutionary growth. They're inherent in our very humanity. Since humans are always growing, the spirals are always there. Since spirals are representative of growth and development, it makes sense that as a human moves forward through the spirals, each spiral takes on a different flavor based on what learning is occurring and has previously occurred.

This spiral progression happens naturally, just as the spiral itself happens naturally. But what if we could define how we grow and develop in time using each spiral as a stepping stone along the way? What if we could not only define growth and observe it as a natural process but also direct it? In this way, we could both sink into the natural cycles that occur involuntarily as we grow as humans and also leverage them and utilize them. We could direct their energy in the direction that we want our growth to go—toward our overarching vision for business, work, or life. What if we could take this development process and direct it to move ourselves, our work, and our offerings to the world toward our vision in a structured way?

In 2009, Roger L. Martin wrote the book *The Design of Business: Why Design Thinking Is the Next Competitive Advantage*. In this book, Martin dives deeply into the progression of development cycles. Design Thinking, as a movement and a philosophy, is closely related to the spiral development process. Since iteration is a foundational principle of Design Thinking, spiral development is a natural match. Design Thinking is an approach for designing new technologies, solutions, and innovations in the business world, but it can be applied to other areas as well, including organizational or personal development. Good design is good design, after all.

In *The Design of Business*, Roger Martin suggests that there are three different stages of knowledge that occur as an individual or organization progresses through subsequent iterations, or spirals. This forms a path made of multiple spirals.

The spiral vortex has three different stages as proposed by Roger Martin: Mystery, Heuristic, and Algorithm.

TIME

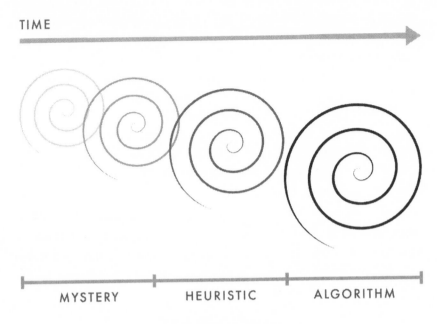

MYSTERY　　　　HEURISTIC　　　　ALGORITHM

Spiral Vortex Stages

Mystery represents the unknown, possibility, risk, innovation, customization, and exploration.

Heuristic, which means "rule of thumb" or "guideline," represents a framework, refinement, focus, adjustment, and mastery.

Algorithm, which means "formula," represents standardization, automation, high reliability, low risk, mass production, and consistency.

To translate Martin's stages into something a little more easily digestible (pun intended), think of it in restaurant terms.

At one end of the restaurant spectrum, you have haute cuisine. It's innovative. It's always new. It's outside the box in flavor combinations, textures, and presentations. Sometimes it's downright weird.

Every plate is customized, or at least blessed, by the chef who conceived it. Usually it's ridiculously expensive, especially compared to the volume of food, but people are willing to pay for the thrill and the specialization. There's high risk—an experimental recipe could completely flop—but it's all part of the show. This, in essence, is Mystery-stage food service.

In the middle of the restaurant spectrum, you have family-owned establishments. The dishes are pretty much what you'd expect: pasta at an Italian place, burritos at a Mexican place, and so on. But each family has its own recipes and secret sauces that make its take on its corner of the food world unique. You always know that you can expect comfort food, but you may develop favorite haunts because they have that one dish you really love. These restaurants are often at a medium price point, but that can range widely depending on the specific parameters of each individual restaurant. That's Heuristic-stage food service.

Then, down at the other end of the restaurant spectrum, you've got fast-food chains. The menus are standardized. The preparation procedures are standardized. Heck, even the food comes standardized off a truck so you know that each item will taste exactly the same as always, no matter where and when you order it. The food process is automated as much as possible to keep human error (and creativity) to a minimum, and the results are not only extremely low risk, but extremely inexpensive. This is Algorithm-stage food service.

I've also seen these stages illustrated beautifully in my own work as an energy industry CEO.

Electrical power has been part of our collective lives since the 1880s. Since that time, electrical utilities have changed little. Their prime objective is to keep your lights on. Innovation within that industry is rare, and risk tolerance is extremely low. Utilities have energy generation and distribution down to a science. The technologies they use to do it haven't changed much in nearly 140 years. They are firmly rooted in the Algorithm stage.

Enter new energy generation technologies, the first disruptors to the industry in a very, very long time. Solar panels, wind turbines, battery energy storage, fuel cells—these innovations promise an energy future that's more economically viable, more sustainable, and better for the planet. But as with all innovation, these technologies haven't been fully explored yet. Solar power, which slowly crept into public consciousness starting in the mid-1970s, is making its way into the Heuristic stage. However, we are still very much in the Mystery stage when it comes to other technologies like large-scale battery storage. Perhaps more importantly, we're deeply in Mystery about how to integrate all of these various generation technologies in distributed or centralized ways and how to take them from hobby status to large, reliable, utility-scale installations.

Because the traditional energy industry—fossil-fuel based, centralized generation administered by utility companies—is so firmly ensconced in the Algorithm stage, it's extremely hard for its players to go back into Mystery and find the creative, outside-the-box ways to integrate new technology. Some people in the industry get caught in the trap of thinking that the new technologies can simply be dropped into the Algorithms—that there are standards, processes, best practices, and reliability in the approach to design, implementation, and deployment of systems, and that those should enable new technology to take root. This is just not the case. At best, forgetting that the new energy industry is in Mystery will result in frustration and lost time and money as new systems run into unexpected challenges. At worst, the industry will miss new, innovative ways to redesign the whole energy infrastructure and create something that maximizes all of this new development.

No single stage of the vortex is more valuable than another. Like the spiral phases, each stage comes with its own set of unique gifts and opportunities. Instead of wishing away the stage you're in, have fun with it and explore it!

The vortex is made up of spirals. Each stage of knowledge maturity may contain one or more spirals, depending on what you're learning about and how complex the subject is.

Let's dive deeper into each of the three stages of the spiral vortex. We're going to walk through each one and discuss what your incremental spirals may look like when you're developing a product or service offering, when you're developing a business or an organization, and when you're working on personal development. Just like the spiral itself, these concepts apply in all domains where there is growth and development. We're going to take the spiral, apply it along the phases of the knowledge vortex, and describe how to use the entire path as a tool to move you forward.

Mystery

TIME

MYSTERY   HEURISTIC   ALGORITHM

In the Mystery stage, you start out asking what kind of problem you're trying to solve. Details are fuzzy, but possibilities are infinite.

At the Mystery stage, you're spending a lot of time asking questions. You're trying to figure out:

- Who am I?

- Why am I here?

- Why am I the right person to do this work?

- Who am I building this for?

- What are the benefits?

- What problem am I trying to solve?

- What are the challenges?

It's when we're in Mystery that we are exploring. It's when we're in Mystery that the great innovations can happen because there is no standard solution. Every single solution is customized.

In my work in the renewable energy field, we help build microgrids, which are collections of energy-generating equipment that are or that can be separated from any main power grid. I was at a technical conference, and I heard Peter Asmuth of Navigate Energy say, "If you've seen one microgrid...you've seen one microgrid." It's not "if you've seen one microgrid, you've seen them all" because no two microgrids are alike. The reason is that, within the energy industry, the integration of renewable and sustainable clean energy resources isn't yet at a place of standardization. The field is young. As an industry, we're in the Mystery phase of the vortex.

Now, you could be in the Mystery phase as an industry. You could be in the Mystery phase as an organization or as an individual. You could be in a Mystery phase just about one particular area, even though other areas are more mature. This is certainly the case in the energy industry, where traditional power companies are pretty much considered to be the opposite of hotbeds of innovation—unlike microgrids, which are metaphorically on fire. At the time of this writing, there are no two microgrids that are alike. Every single microgrid solution is completely custom. Every single solution requires lots of human intervention, lots of human brainpower to make things work in each specific situation.

When you're at the Mystery stage of the vortex, innovation and development of new ideas are more expensive. They're more expensive in terms of the time that needs to be spent to develop them and the brainpower that needs to go into them. So, those solutions developed during the Mystery phase are going to be more expensive.

This is why new technologies on the market start out at an expensive price point, which only a few early adopters are willing to pay. Then, slowly (or not so slowly) they come down in price and become affordable for the mass market. Then, as there is widespread adoption of the new technology (and the bugs get worked out), the technology, process, and approach become standardized, which enables the price to drop in both time and financial investments.

The same thing is true if you're developing any kind of product or service to offer in business. You're developing an innovation, a new way to look at a problem and solve it. You're necessarily starting out in the Mystery stage, in at least some aspect, otherwise it wouldn't be innovative. The first time that you go around that spiral, it's definitely about Mystery, and it's not necessarily about finding solutions. It's about asking the right questions.

The Mystery stage might not be restricted to that first time around the spiral. It might take several spirals to get through the Mystery stage. It might take several spirals to get through any of the vortex stages. So often, we are focused on driving ourselves through these knowledge stages as quickly as possible, but that's not necessarily the most beneficial thing. In the Mystery phase, for example, there is so much opportunity for innovation. If you rush by that, you lose your power to be truly disruptive. You'd have to go all the way back to the drawing board, when anything is possible. Toss out everything you thought you knew, and try it again from scratch.

Critical to the Mystery stage are the Inspiration and Introspection phases of the spiral. Those are the yin side, the feminine side, the flow side of the spiral. Those are the phases of disruptive innovation, which is aligned with Mystery. The major functions in those phases are critical pieces of the Mystery stage, even though you'll still work through the other side of the spiral.

The Implementation and Investigation phases are how you progress out of the Mystery stage and into the Heuristic stage. You'll progress through the spiral vortex by going out and doing something, by gathering data, and by getting your work in front of people. You have to take action in order to figure out who you are going to be. You have to build momentum. The action-taking phases of the spiral in the Mystery stage provide the momentum you need to be agile. These help you change your creative direction and steer the ship, which is a good thing in the Mystery stage at a time when your strategic vision is (or should be) highly adaptable.

Taking brave action in the face of so many unknowns and being constantly prepared to reshape the plan can cause consternation. The not-knowing can cause frustration. You may not really know how to articulate what you're trying to accomplish, and you may not even really know how to think about yourself and what you're trying to do. It feels like an identity crisis—you don't really know who you are.

In reality, if you can flip the feeling from "frustrated by not having answers" to "exploring all the many possibilities," you just might find something that looks a lot like joy. It's playtime. Give yourself the space to have fun and experiment. You'll find that in creating space for play, you will have naturally created the space in which you can generate the momentum to keep yourself and your venture moving forward.

The Mystery Stage for Product Development

If you're developing a product or service, you start out by asking, "What problem am I going to solve for the client?" or perhaps, "How can I help the client?" Once you start to answer those questions, you can start to rough in what that solution looks like. You could employ some Design Thinking concepts and consider the use cases. You could ask, "What is the client doing now to solve this problem, and why doesn't that solution work? How can I develop something better?"

This is where innovation comes from. You're looking for that opportunity to do something in a better way. To do that, you ask lots of questions. How do your superpowers, your skills, gifts, talents, and passions come together in a way that's going to solve this problem in a different way for your people?

Example: The Architect Your Business Course

I knew that I wanted to help my clients craft a solid, comprehensive business vision that was also flexible. This was the problem I wanted to solve.

I'd seen other business development and marketing gurus talk about doing this. They said, "Just follow my step-by-step process, and you'll be making six figures by next week." The hyperbole drove me up a wall. I had taken some of these courses. I had seen my friends and colleagues take some of these courses. It's crap, right? You're not going to make six figures next week. Even if you follow their step-by-step process, it might not go well for you. These programs demonstrate the myth of linearity. If you did follow their step-by-step process, and you didn't get their predicted result, well, you were just out of luck. These methods didn't provide any way to iterate. At the time, this was the available solution, which I found to be lacking.

Instead, I wanted to make sure that people were able to craft a strong yet flexible vision. I wanted to help clients take all of their biggest, pie-in-the-sky, ten-year-business-plan dreams and be able to distill that big-picture vision into practical, actionable terms. I wanted them to answer the question, "How do I make money as soon as possible so that I'm sustaining myself and my life while I'm still moving toward my bigger dreams?" These were the questions I was asking as I started to develop my *Architect Your Business* course. These questions framed the innovative solution that I wanted to deliver.

I didn't necessarily know how I was going to do all that at the beginning, but I knew I probably could. Also, I wanted to be able to drive some revenue for my own business along the way, even though I didn't have all the answers in a "proven system" up front.

In my first time around the spiral—the Mystery spiral—I designed a customized, pay-what-you-can service offering that was available for a limited time. It was a two-hour power coaching session with me to develop business architecture. I let clients pay as little as ten dollars and as much as they wanted. There were people who paid me amounts all across the spectrum to do this, so I did drive some revenue.

In the Investigation phase, I sat down with the clients individually for two hours, and I let them brain dump everything in their head about their business: how they were feeling stuck, what their dreams were, and what their superpowers were. Perhaps they never wanted to offer one-on-one coaching or consulting, but they really liked the idea of putting on retreats. Perhaps they had no interest in writing a book but were intrigued by podcasting. They had all of these different ideas for the "what," but they didn't know how to put it together in an order that made sense.

I listened to each individual and asked some clarifying questions. When we were done with the session, I took all of my notes and compiled them into a 10- to 15-page document summarizing in a professional and structured manner everything we'd discussed. I also suggested some next steps they could take to start putting this vision into place. I sometimes filled in some of the gaps for them using my own ideas. But mostly, it was simply an organized reflection back of what they'd told me.

I had about 20 clients sign up for this service. By the time I got to client number 12, I found that I was writing the same headings in the deliverable document. I was asking the same questions of clarification. I had naturally and accidentally developed a template. My template was in a mostly standardized form with a very few exceptions for a few outliers. That right there was the gateway to the Heuristic stage. I started to have some rules of thumb about the questions I needed to ask and the format of the deliverable that would maximize value for my clients.

That was the first spiral—the Mystery spiral—of my product development.

If you're working on product development, my question for you right now is "What's in your Mystery spiral?" What are the questions you need to ask to develop an innovative and unique solution for your clients? What are the unknowns that you're okay living with while getting in front of clients? How can you start from where you are right now?

If you look back at my Mystery spiral, you can see each distinct phase. I had to conceive of the idea, be inspired, and activate that spiral by saying, "This is what I'm going to help people with. I want to help people craft this flexible vision for their business, but one that has practical results so that they can actually make money. And I'm going to do it differently from the way all the other business-training gurus do it." That was the Inspiration phase.

The Implementation phase was where I was actually putting the offering together. I started to say, "This is how I'm actually, specifically going to do it. I'm going to have a two-hour coaching session, and I'm going to use the session to put together this document." And I set up all the logistics around my very simple marketing plan: taking payment, conducting the sessions, and gathering feedback.

Then I came around into the Investigation phase, where I actually did the work with clients and delivered results. When I was willing to be vulnerable and say, "Hey, you know, I'm human. I'm making this up as I go along, but I think I can help," that's where the magic happened. This was not a standardized product. This was me talking to individuals—person to person, human to human. I did my best to solve their specific problems with a customized solution because I was in the Mystery phase. I was okay with the flexibility of not having a formulaic process, and they got the benefit of not being crammed into a generic solution.

After that Investigation phase, and before I moved into the Heuristic stage of the spiral vortex, I went through Introspection. I went back, looked at my template, and made sure that I could create something useful from it. I'd taken feedback— both from clients and from myself—as to what had gone right and what had gone wrong. Some of that feedback turned into social proof (like testimonials) for the next phase of development. Then, I was able to move into spiral two, the Heuristic spiral.

The Mystery Stage for Business Development

For developing a business or organization, the same pattern holds true, but on a slightly larger scale. During the Mystery stage of any business or organization, you may not have completely standard offerings. You may not even have a solid grasp on who you are trying to be yet, and that's okay. As a business, you may be focused more on offering consulting or custom solutions as opposed to standardized products, apps, software, or programs that may come in the later phases. (Anytime you get software involved, it's by definition an Algorithm. In order to have software, there is an Algorithm of some sort that underpins it.) Instead, you might work with clients on an individual, customized level, or on a case-by-case basis. You develop custom solutions. You're still trying to figure out who you are, and that's okay.

You might start down a few paths that you're not sure you want to continue on. You might start down one and end up saying, "Well, that didn't work out very well. I don't really want to continue in that line of business." Perfect! That's a great answer to come to during the Mystery stage when you're exploring! It's not a good question to answer during the Algorithm stage when you've already gotten a standardized product line.

"Fail fast and fail often" is the mantra of the Mystery stage of the spiral vortex when you're a business owner or an organizational leader. Because you're in this stage, you're allowing yourself the flexibility to take more risks, be more exploratory, do more custom work, and not worry about it so much.

Since you're in a stage of risk tolerance, you can be more innovative. You can be more daring with solutions and with ideas. You can foster the kind of culture where no idea is a bad idea. You can allow brainstorming and inspiration to come into the workplace.

The Mystery Stage for Personal Development

At the macro level, you might think of your own personal development as linear. You know it's not totally linear because you go through spirals, and you've identified with the spiral phases we just talked about. But you might think that every spiral comes around and moves you consistently forward. You're on this monotonically increasing growth path, right?

No. Because humans love new experiences. Part of growth and change is stepping into the discomfort of something new. There are always going to be new things in life, whether that's my grandma learning to use a computer, someone taking up a new sport or hobby, or someone moving to a new location and needing to develop a new social circle.

Lots of starting over happens in life. Every time you try something new, you're going back to the drawing board, which means—you guessed it—you are returning to the Mystery phase.

This is the time to ask questions. This is the time to go back and say, "What do I really want here? What am I really offering to this planet, to this global consciousness? And then, as I go around the spiral, and I'm looking to do something— to create something with my life, with my work, with my family—what does that look like? How can I have fun with it? How can I play with it? And if I'm not an expert yet in whatever I'm pursuing here, that's just fine, because I'm just trying some things out, and I'm trying to decide if I do want to be an expert. I'm trying to decide if I do want to refine and hone my skills in the future."

Allow yourself to go around those initial spirals and to explore. Allow yourself let go of worry about having to have a routine, making it standardized, or doing it the same way it's always been done. There's a time and a place for standardization, routine, and tradition (ahem, the Algorithm stage), and there is comfort in those things. But there's excitement and inspiration in trying something new. It's adventure—and a regular return to Mystery—that keeps you young.

Personal development is the area in which it's perhaps most important to remind yourself that you're in Mystery. You don't have to have it all figured out yet.

We humans can be really hard on ourselves. We tend to think (for some reason) that we should have instant mastery, instant expertise, just because we did something once. At least, that's the way my brain works.

Giving yourself the grace to experience the Mystery stage is a blessing. Giving yourself the grace of empty space to explore what's unknown is a blessing. How comfortable are you with what's unknown? The unknown is the excitement of Mystery. That's when the ideas flow. That's when you discover the purpose for the next phase of your life.

Allow yourself to be in Mystery until you have experimented enough to find the thing that you're ready to take forward. At that point, you're ready to move to the Heuristic stage.

Heuristic

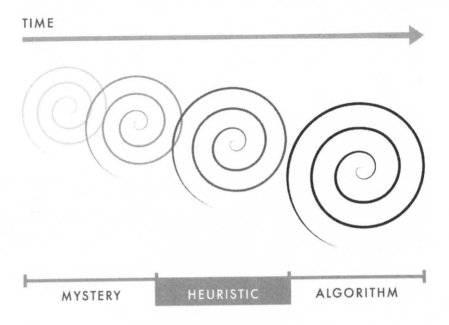

TIME

MYSTERY — HEURISTIC — ALGORITHM

The second stage of the spiral vortex is Heuristic, which means "rule of thumb." You've moved out of the stage of Mystery, and by extension, the phase of disruptive innovation. After you've exited the Mystery stage, you're starting to develop a solid feel for what you are doing and where you are headed with it. The chaos may feel as if it's settling down a bit. You're able to derive rules of thumb about how you operate, about what your solution does, about what your business provides, and about how you're showing up in the world. The rules-of-thumb stage is a powerful place to be because you're able to take all of the custom, detailed work that you did in the Mystery phase and integrate it into guiding principles.

Your rules of thumb guide you. What does that guidance do? It speeds up your process. It takes out some of the bumps in the road. You've developed some intuition from lessons you've learned. You can say, "Yeah, I've been to this rodeo before. I kind of know what the challenges are and how the process works. Generally speaking, I know what's going to help people and what won't." You're able to grow your audience, your influence, or your scope. You're also able to better articulate what you do because it's easy to sum it up in general terms. If the Mystery stage is about innovation, the Heuristic stage is about refinement.

You're really in it now.

The Heuristic Stage for Product Development

As you're going through the Heuristic stage, you take what you did in Mystery and refine it. That could mean that you're adding to it. You could be adding material. You could be adding features. It could mean that you're expanding the scope. Instead of serving just a few people with custom solutions, you're able to serve more people or a group all at once by moving toward standardization. It's not completely codified yet, but you're comfortable enough with your solution that things start to feel a little easier.

As you develop rules of thumb and guidelines, you're able to refine how you show up. You're able to refine the offering. You're able to refine the messaging in a way that's going to help you clarify who you are, what you're doing, and what you have to offer.

In the Heuristic phase, the Introspection piece is critical because you need to look back at Mystery and say, "Okay. How do we move this forward?" You'll need to get inspired just enough to take the framework that you already have and refine it. But the magic of the Heuristic stage is in the Implementation. You're taking the Inspiration and the lessons learned from the Mystery stage and truly making something amazing with it. This is where the real work gets done—where you start to build something that's going to stand the test of time.

Mystery is where you laid the foundation for this real work. You can't have skipped over the exploration that happens in Mystery if you are going to build something really impactful. Those marketing gurus who say you're going to make six figures next week? They're not going to tell you this part. They tell you to have the idea for your course or your training or your offering in the first week of their course, and then to build it during the second week. They ask you to skip a major part of the creative process, which is to explore the Mystery stage before diving into the build. If you've invested the time in the Mystery stage, you've dived deeply into your own innovation and creativity, and you've tested your ideas while collecting some data. You have done the work that gives you the foundation you need to build something lasting.

Now in the Heuristic stage, you're set to create something that's production ready. You don't need to spend so much time fooling around with crazy and high-risk ideas. You're able to serve more people and to think about scaling. Your work here is integrated and solid in a way that reflects your deepest-rooted superpowers. You can be confident that you are truly addressing the challenges of your clients. You know this because you've gotten your work in front of them already. That's the beauty of the Heuristic stage.

Example: The Architect Your Business Course

In our case study, which is my *Architect Your Business* course, the Mystery stage consisted of individual coaching sessions with customized business architectures that I created for each specific client. By the end of the Mystery stage, I had developed a template.

I knew what questions I asked of nearly everybody. In the Introspection phase of the Mystery spiral, I noticed there were two people for whom I had developed a completely custom solution, totally different from the others. One was trying to develop multiple businesses, and one was in a completely different field from all the others. Looking at the data during the Introspection phase enabled me to say, "I'm going to call those people outliers. I'm not going to design a standardized solution for them." I set those cases aside.

Then, I took my now-standard template, and I said, "Eventually, I want people to be able to lead themselves through this. I'm looking ahead toward the Algorithm phase." That was the big idea—I wanted a program that people could go through themselves without any intervention from me. I had to ask myself, "How do I take the template that I developed in my customized Mystery offerings and move it to a totally automated Algorithm-stage course in the final stage of development?"

The gap between those states is the Heuristic stage.

I started to develop the course material that would eventually become the automated course. I offered it to clients as a group coaching program with lots of involvement from me so that I could guide and shape the process. I was still interacting with individuals, but I did it in a group setting. I started to transfer the work from me to them. The major difference between the Mystery stage and the Heuristic stage was that I wasn't going to do the work for them. I was going to lead them through the process of doing the work for themselves.

With the help of my small group of clients, I refined the template into a course. I asked them the same questions I'd asked in my custom sessions, and then I gave them the space to find their own answers. I developed the course material: the worksheets, the lessons, and the video training modules that were going to become the course foundation. As I led the group program, we got together weekly to talk about the course material, and I engaged with participants daily in a Facebook group, so they had lots of support from me.

The actual execution of the group program was the Investigation phase of the Heuristic spiral. I still gathered feedback about the content, but I also wanted to know about logistics: the usability; the human factors of how they're engaging; the user experience of working with the course, the website, and the course materials. That was the key feedback from my Heuristic stage.

Once I integrated that feedback, I had a body of work that was ready to be deployed in a standardized course format with refined user experience. That put me at the gateway of the Algorithm stage.

If you've done some exploring and playing around with what you might want to offer, enough to have thrown it out there in front of people, you've completed the Mystery stage. You have the general idea of how to solve the problems of your clients. You've basically seen enough clients that you're feeling confident that you have a solution that works. You'd be able to standardize this and make it scalable. You're in the Heuristic phase. So, now I'm going to ask you to think about how you can bridge that gap between your initial brilliant idea, which has already been proven, and something that's scalable, standardized, and, perhaps, passive. Whatever Algorithm looks like for you, how do you bridge the gap between Mystery and Algorithm? That's your quest as you develop a product or service offering in the Heuristic stage.

The Heuristic Stage for Business Development

Similarly, if you're looking at your overall business development and entering the Heuristic stage, you're in that sweet spot where you still have some wiggle room in which to innovate, be dynamic, and play. But you're also starting to feel the relief of having a handle on what it is you're doing. You've done enough in your business or organization so you can articulate clearly what you're offering and who you're offering it to.

You've got your elevator pitch down snappy, and you're really comfortable with it. The elevator pitch comes into its own during the Heuristic stage because your elevator pitch is itself a rule of thumb about what your business does and who you help. You have a crisp mission statement. You have crisp core company values or organizational values. You have a crisp strategic vision. All of these things are coming into sharp focus, so you're able to articulate them clearly through your messaging and branding. If you're in the Heuristic stage of business development, it's a great time to work on your messaging, marketing, and outreach strategy.

Instead of investing a lot of time figuring out who you are, you're going to go around the spiral again thinking about how you interact with the outside world. Whereas the Mystery stage is inward-looking, the Heuristic stage is focused outward. You are starting to ask what the venues are in which you interact to attract your perfect clients and gain business. You're learning more about your clients. You're learning what type of marketing works and what type doesn't. You're also close enough to Mystery that if you have more innovative ideas, they can still be incorporated.

The Heuristic stage is this great middle ground, bridging the gap between a venture that's totally new, innovative, and unknown, and a venture that's completely defined and understood.

The Heuristic Stage for Personal Development

Personal development is about learning new things and making changes in your life. This is something that happens naturally, for sure. But we humans are anxious and hurried, and sometimes we rush the normal learning and growth processes. Knowing the stages of the spiral vortex can help you remember that you are on track— that you are nowhere else but exactly where you should be. As with the phases of the spiral, giving yourself grace to spend time in each vortex stage, and not wishing for the other stages past or future, is critical.

If you've gone through one or more spirals in the Mystery stage, you've been trying to figure something out. You're at the threshold of change. You're figuring out who you are, who you want to be, and what you want to try. You're open to experimentation.

By the time you get to the Heuristic stage of personal development, you've gotten the hang of some things. You have some rules of thumb to go by. You have some guidelines. You know that if you work out after 5:00 p.m., you won't sleep from the endorphins. You know you should stop drinking coffee at 3:00 p.m. Those aren't hard-and-fast rules; they're rules of thumb. Those are guidelines to help you live a happy, healthy life. And you're pretty clear about the consequences of breaking the rules.

You're in the sweet spot here because you're not feeling so confused and frustrated by your lack of knowledge, and you're pretty sure you know about the things you still have to figure out. You feel comfortable because you can make plans and execute on them.

As I said before, the key spiral phase in the Heuristic stage is Implementation. You've got your bearings. You're clear on what you need and want. Now it's time to buckle down and put the scaffolding you need in place. It's time to build.

You're losing that feeling of thrashing around so much and gaining a calmer, more centered feeling. You're not expending so much energy trying to figure yourself out. Now, use all of your energy to create the life you want and develop the skills you need. This is where you get to actually make it happen.

Algorithm

TIME

MYSTERY   HEURISTIC   ALGORITHM

The third and final stage of the spiral vortex is Algorithm, which is about standardization and repeatability. This is where you actually get to say, "Well, if you've seen one [fill in the blank], you've seen them all." Your understanding of the situation is so deep that you've got things down to a science. You're in a rhythm. This can be true in business or in your personal life.

You don't need to change much at this point. You don't need to do experiments to see if something else works for you because you know what works. You've got an Algorithm—a formula. You just need to execute it, and you don't have to think about it.

The downside of being in the Algorithm stage is that there is zero innovation. But the corresponding beauty of this stage is that you start to take your brain out of the loop; you don't have to think so hard. You don't have to expend mental energy on every single thing. As a result, you're able to scale up or turn your attention elsewhere.

A lot of people get obsessed with this standardized Algorithm phase because they want to be able to scale up. They tend to rush straight past the innovation and refinement parts. They forget about the power in these other two phases. Don't do that.

In a lot of ways, Algorithm is the goal, especially in a business context. It may be the goal in your personal life so that you can free your brain to go back to the beginning of some other problem and look for another Mystery to solve. Or, it may not be the goal if you just enjoy the variety and challenge of problem solving and trying things out.

The purpose of getting to the Algorithm stage is to release that particular vortex so that you can come back around to the beginning and start a new one. It's like a metaspiral. You step through these three stages and then spiral back to the beginning of the vortex at the Mystery stage on some other problem to start the growth adventure all over again.

Before that beautiful turning of the wheel can happen, you have to make sure that whatever you've been working on is fully moved up into the Algorithm stage of the knowledge vortex.

The Algorithm Stage for Product Development

The key to moving a product or service to the Algorithm stage is scalability. You're trying to reach lots and lots of people. You're also thinking about taking customization or individualization, including much (if not all) of the human interaction, out of the process, making it automated or passive. Passivity, automation, and standardization are all keys to scalability. Will you still offer custom solutions? Of course you will. But those custom solutions are going to draw a higher price point than a standardized, mass-produced solution because they're going to demand more interaction from you (like haute cuisine as opposed to fast food, right?).

Once you have a product standardized, it can be presented to a wider audience because of its repeatability. It can also be presented at a lower price point that's more accessible to a wider audience.

Example: The Architect Your Business Course

Once I completed *Architect Your Business* in the group coaching program format, I was ready to drop back into the Introspection phase of the spiral. What I got out of that Introspection was that I had a pretty solid course. What remained for me to put in place to get to Algorithm, was the course automation. I also tweaked a few pieces of content in response to feedback. The Inspiration phase of the Algorithm spiral wasn't particularly innovative. It was about filling in the gaps in logistics to automate the sales and course experiences and figuring out how to remove myself from the process.

Then, in the Implementation phase, it was just a matter of putting all the pieces into place. A lot of box-checking happened: a landing page, a funnel, a sales page, a payment gateway, and connecting the course website and registration to an email sequence designed to "drip" the course to participants.

For the Investigation phase, I simply launched. I opened up the cart and let people in. At that point, my trip through the spiral vortex was complete for the *Architect Your Business* course.

I was able to release my product into the world as a full-fledged, self-guided course and passive income stream that was totally automated. I was able to offer the automated course at a lower price point than private coaching, which made it accessible a wider range of people. The course is still operating. Since the course is set up to run on its own, I only have to worry about routine maintenance.

Completing the spiral vortex for this product freed up my brain-power to go back to my overarching business vision and say, "What's next? What am I going to go after next? What am I going to explore in the Mystery phase next?" Then I was able to start all over again. That's what you can do too.

Getting to Algorithm was enabled by the time and effort I invested in the Mystery and Heuristic stages. I wouldn't have been able to jump from the first "business architecture" idea I had straight to a fully automated course. I certainly wouldn't have been able to do it with confidence. Allowing my product to develop iteratively and putting it in front of real clients at several points along the way validated my ideas and approach and made my final product (and the associated marketing) robust. What's more, it made it easy to get to Algorithm when the time finally came.

This whole process took me about six months from the conception of the idea to the launch of the automated course. The timeline for your product development vortex is totally dependent upon what you are building. It could take a month. It could take a year or more. But no matter how long it takes, when you allow your ideas to unfold naturally, you are able to go through the process with joy, wonder, and ease.

If you're sitting at the gateway between Heuristic and Algorithm, it's time to think about what scalability looks like. It might look like an automated product offering, similar to *Architect Your Business*. It could look like a software platform or an app. It may look like a device or piece of equipment. It may just look like periodic group programs or retreats that you run in a standardized way every single time so that it's formulaic.

I want you to think about what scalability, standardization, and automation mean to you, and how you can minimize your work on this product so you can free up your brain to go work on your next big thing and dive back into Mystery.

The Algorithm Stage for Business Development

If you're in a business, the Algorithm stage is all about reliability. It's all about staying extremely low risk by doing your thing the same way every time. Think assembly line. Think standard processes and procedures. Think best practices. Think ISO certification or any number of business standards, depending on your industry. Now, some of that might sound boring to you. But in some ways, this is living the dream—if you can be so low-risk and so reliable that you can have this level of stability. Algorithm means stability.

If you're knocking on the door of the Algorithm stage of business development, what I want you to really think about is how you can minimize human input into the processes that need to happen to keep your business running. By taking human input out, you free up brainpower to solve more problems and develop new ideas on your own or with your team. That should be the goal of any Algorithm stage at an organizational level.

Reliability is all well and good, but growth, change, and innovation are essential to the health of any business and organization. While we're all pursuing the Algorithm stage because of its scalability, reach, and accessibility, the ultimate goal of the Algorithm stage for a business or an organization is to free up human brainpower to solve new problems.

That's how you find the happy medium between reliability and in-novation. That's how you keep the spark of Inspiration alive.

Let that be your goal.

The Algorithm Stage for Personal Development

Algorithms for your personal life are beautiful things. They are pro-cesses that you don't have to spend any brainpower figuring out. They're habits—good ones, I hope. They're rituals. They are things that you do morning and night. Some personal Algorithms may include keeping a gratitude journal, writing down your objectives for the day, having an evening reflection time, doing weekly planning, doing your grocery shopping once every three weeks. Your rhythms, your daily rituals, your periodic activities are just Algorithms in your daily life.

You don't have to think about how to make coffee. You do it by rote. You know exactly how your machine works. You know exactly how you like it. You rarely vary it. There is comfort and stability in that sameness. And that frees your brain to think about your plans for the coming day, which might vary, while you're still getting the coffee ready.

A friend of mine suffered from a traumatic brain injury. While she was recovering, she called me in a panic and said, "I can't even remember how to make my coffee!"

I told her, "Don't feel guilty about not being able to remember. Write down the procedure on a little index card, tape it on the wall next to the coffee maker, and just read the procedure every morning. You don't have to be so hard on yourself." If you can't keep an Algorithm, routine, or ritual in your brain, write it down. There's no reason to take up brain space with it. These are the habits and the routines that free us up to go do something amazing. To do something creative and innovative where it really counts.

If you have habits, rituals, and routines that help you accomplish all of your mundane tasks in a reliable, secure, comfortable way, it frees up your brain and your energy to be creative, to be an artist, to solve problems, and to handle challenges that come along your way. That's the beauty of the Algorithm phase.

If you are in the Algorithm phase of personal development, what you've really been working on is standardizing procedures in your everyday life. Everything may feel, well, boring. If that's the case, please remember that the point of the Algorithm stage is not to stay stuck in standardization. The point of the Algorithm stage is to free your brain up to go do something else. To do something exciting. Algorithm provides you with the grounding, structural framework of habits and rituals and routines that you can rely upon so that you can go out and be innovative. You can go out and grow, change, learn new things, and impact your world because you have this solid foundation.

You may feel that as you're coming out of the Heuristic stage, you have these rules of thumb to live by, and you're getting the hang of it, but it's still challenging. In that case, what you're looking for is how to plug these rules of thumb into routines, rituals, or habits to make them standardized. That's going to give you that solid foundation from which you can step into your full power.

PART IV: PRACTICE

CHAPTER SIXTEEN

Innovate or Perish

IF YOU'VE WORKED IN THE CORPORATE WORLD for any length of time, you may have heard the phrase "innovate or perish." That seems like a very drastic and overly dramatic statement to make, but think of it from an organizational standpoint. Think about a gigantic, monolithic legacy corporation. The founders probably started with an innovative idea. But, over the years, as they've progressed through their own version of the spiral vortex from Mystery to Heuristic to Algorithm, they've valued innovation less and less. They've lost their tolerance for risk, and they've come to value reliability more and more.

As we slip into the comfort and security of doing things the way they've always been done, we get to the point where innovation isn't just uncommon but is outright rejected. Innovative solutions are viewed as too risky, too outside the box, too wild. Meanwhile, the world moves on. Individuals, organizations, and culture as a whole continue to spiral, to be inspired, to create new things. And these large, monolithic organizations that can't adapt—and reject innovation out of hand—slowly (or sometimes not so slowly) start to die from the inside out.

Our own individual, internal voices of fear prefer the apparent security of reliability. They believe there's safety in routine and in doing things the way they've always been done. While the risk of starting or trying something new can feel exciting and adventurous, it can also trigger fear. Your voice of fear cries out in protest, "Hey! What gives? Things were *fine* the way they were. Why would I want to make changes?"

The spiral is there whether you like it or not. You can choose to engage with it and deliberately move with it, or you can fight it. If you adamantly resist the creative spiral, that's when you start to run into friction, pain, and misalignment. The spiral *is* the creative process, the factory of innovation, the engine of growth. If you are alive, you are spiraling. If you are resisting the spiral, you are resisting your very humanity. You're resisting growth itself.

Football coach Lou Holtz famously said, "In this world you're either growing or you're dying, so get in motion and grow." Since the spiral is the engine of growth, you may just as well say, "You're either *spiraling* or you're dying." We have to be engaging with these evolutionary growth cycles, willing to allow them to happen in order to be growing and not dying.

There are seasons of life or work during which you may want to actively push forward through the spiral phases. There may also be times when you gently, quietly allow the spiral to take its course, accepting the gifts of each phase while you release the last. In either case, whether you take a more active or passive approach to leveraging the spiral path, you allow the natural cycle to happen.

Things start to break down when you firmly plant your feet and say, "I do not need this next phase. I firmly resist the voice of Inspiration." Or "I firmly resist the need to rest, rejuvenate, and reevaluate." Resistance to the natural flow of your own evolutionary growth induces stress responses that you then pack away into different parts of your body. These stored stresses come back to haunt you as your body stores and processes the stress that it was never meant to handle. Your body breaks down and you get sick. You are, in a very real and physical sense, dying.

You may agree and say, "For sure—innovate or perish. Allow the spirals to happen." But it can be easier said than done. There's an element of our primal brains that prefers the reliability of doing things the way they've always been done, of counting on the routines, of not trying things that are new because they seem scary or high risk. Some of us are better at overcoming this primal impulse than others.

How do you set yourself up for success? How do you set yourself up to be able to engage with the spiral either in a deliberate, forward-pushing sort of way or in a receptive, flowing sort of way? How do you engage with the spiral so that you're able to keep growing and moving forward instead of being stuck, being stagnant, and, yes, dying?

CHAPTER SEVENTEEN

Vision

THE SPIRAL IS AN INFINITE JOURNEY, so where do we start, practically speaking?

We always begin with vision. A good vision is the glue that holds everything together, even if you tend toward the "go with the flow" side most of the time.

I always prefer the word *vision* to *goals*.

We are taught and then conditioned from a very young age to make our goals SMART: Specific, Measurable, Achievable, Realistic, and Time-bound. These qualities involve quantitative measures of success. While there's certainly a time and a place for quantitative measures of success in very specific instances, in many cases, such numbers are selected arbitrarily and force an unwarranted sense of failure (or, indeed, success), and they become a false representation of progress (or lack thereof). For example, if an individual sets a SMART goal to lose 20 pounds by February 1st, and she loses 18 pounds instead, is she considered a failure? How about if she loses 20 pounds by February 15th instead? Any rational person will say that this goal-setter was successful in getting healthier, looking more svelte, and feeling great in her own skin. These were the underlying success criteria, but since they aren't SMART, they are rejected in favor of arbitrary numbers.

To take the example one step further, this wellness goal-setter may, in fact, feel a certain sense of failure having not met the quantitative measure set forth in the SMART goal. That failure mindset can have far-reaching effects: feeling as though future health and wellness efforts are futile, continuing to have negative thoughts about her body (even though the underlying success criteria were achieved), and even feeling "not good enough" in other aspects of life as this sense of failure spreads and infects her general approach toward other projects. It can even affect her general sense of self. Insidious, isn't it? An innocent little number, chosen haphazardly, can cause so much damage.

(Don't get me started on the cultural addiction to numbers on the scale or on the tags in pants, both of which have relatively nothing to do with overall health. But I digress.)

This numbers-only mindset is equally true in business, where we are bombarded with income levels as a success criterion (six- or seven-figure business, anyone?) and the number of mailing list subscribers and social media followers as a definitive measure of impact and influence. It's deemed even better if these measures occur within an inordinately short period of time. We have this tendency to believe that a person who achieved six figures in an overnight success story is somehow more successful than a person who built a foundation over several years.

Numbers and timelines can, of course, be extremely useful and important in very specific situations. And data and analysis of results can be powerful tools to help you understand the underlying mechanisms of what's happening (we'll talk about those later as another form of structure). But in terms of choosing the target for where you want to go, be wary of arbitrarily selecting numbers just because you think you should.

Setting a goal is like using GPS turn-by-turn directions. It's a prescriptive solution. You dial in the very specific destination for which you're aiming, and then you blindly follow a single route to get there. You have no external knowledge to tell you about the accident that just happened along your route (even in the post-Waze era) or if there's a different route just a couple of minutes longer that is significantly more scenic and enjoyable. And you keep your head down, following your phone, doing exactly what it says, to the exclusion of all other sources of information, including your own five senses.

A vision, on the other hand, is like using a map and a trail or travel guide. The map gives you context for what is all around you. You get to use your own five senses and your own desires, even as they change, to choose the routes that make the most sense for you at any given time. You get to choose if you want to challenge yourself with the harder route. You get to choose if you want to take a detour to a scenic waterfall for a lunch stop. The structure of the vision gives you information that complements your own senses, intuition, and desires. The structure of the vision still supports you as you change your mind.

A vision is a painted picture of what you are headed toward. Instead of arbitrarily using numbers to define the target, the target is imagery or narrative that invokes emotions that you hold to be important for your overall sense of success and happiness.

A vision is adaptable and easy to evolve as you grow and learn about what works and what doesn't, and as you refine your business concept through time and experience.

So, what's in a vision? There are two main components:

- Who you want to be?

- What you want to do?

Being

Dr. Wayne Dyer rocked my world when I heard him say, "You're a human *being* not a human *doing*." It took me years to wrap my arms around the difference between who I am (or want to be) and what I do (or want to do). But I think the distinction between *being* and *doing* is key to crafting a complete vision, no matter how simple or complex.

Your values form the foundation of your vision. Your values express qualities that are important to you. How do you want to be? Generous? A good leader? Recognized and acclaimed? Peaceful? Of service to others? These are your values, your highest aims as an individual.

The second component of the *being* side of your vision is what I call your superpower(s). Gay Hendricks called it your "zone of genius." It's your own *je ne sais quoi* in how you go about the world (which actually makes it hard for me to define for you, and also hard for most of us to articulate for ourselves). It's the thing you do that feels magical to you and looks magical to others. It's what you innately bring to any situation. It's not related to a job, an industry, or a topic area. It's not really related to what you do because you bring it to whatever you do, whether that's raising tiny awesome humans, building a world-changing business, or leading a movement.

These are the main components that I include in the *being* side of vision. You might have more, and that would be just fine. But ultimately, you need to answer the question "How do you want to be?"

Doing

What you want to do may look like a job title, a manner of working, a lifestyle you want to live, an industry, or a mission. These are accomplishments that are easy to turn into goals because they're more concrete than the components of *being*. When you talk about what you want to do, usually it's easy to map out the general path toward that end.

All of this combines to make your vision. If you are living in service to your values and utilizing your superpowers (and applying them to activities you love, find fun, and believe in), you can't help but be happy, confident, fulfilled, and hopeful. These positive emotions result from the integration of *being* and *doing*, which forms the vision.

This format describes a vision whether you are an individual or a business, by the way. Values can be defined for a company as well as for an individual. Superpowers can reflect the fact that the whole of an organization is greater than the sum of its parts. And obviously, a business can carry a mission and/or vision statement defining its *do*-based objectives. So, although a vision can feel like a really personal thing, I highly recommend this format at the business or organizational level as well.

"How do I know my vision is developed enough?" is a common question that comes up with my coaching clients. Your vision can be as detailed or as nebulous as you want it to be, as long as it's serving you in your enterprise. I find that the specificity of the vision is directly related to what stage of the spiral vortex you're in.

If you are in the Mystery stage, your vision is necessarily going to be vaguer and more nebulous than if you are in Heuristic or Algorithm. You don't know what you're doing yet, and that's fine! The whole point of the Mystery stage is the exploration of the unknown. Of course you aren't going to have a terribly specific vision if you have only a basic idea of who you want to be or what you want to offer.

As you move through Heuristic and Algorithm, you start to get really specific about what you want (and what you don't want). Your vision is super specific because it can be.

Don't be fooled by the SMART-goal apologists! You can ride for years on a vision that's just a vague picture of something you'd like to do someday, even if the *how* is totally obscured for you. That's enough to get started! Have faith that, as you evolve naturally out of Mystery, the vision and the path will become clearer.

Remember that a vision is supposed to change. No matter what stage of the vortex you're in, a vision is pliable. You are an ever-evolving creature. Your business is an ever-evolving organism. And your vision is just an extension of those things. The Introspection phase of the spiral is a great time to step back from the specifics of the projects you're working on and step into the big picture of your vision.

Sometimes, your vision might simply need tweaking based on what you've learned in your spirals. But don't be afraid to occasionally question everything. Sometimes, the whole vision needs an overhaul. I think that the identity crisis I faced when I left spacecraft design was mostly caused by the fact that I expected my vision for life and work to remain the same throughout my life. I mistook strength of vision for staying power. And I don't mean that in a bad way. I just didn't comprehend the inevitability of change and growth—first within myself, and then, consequently, within my vision.

How do you know when it's time to adjust or overhaul your vision? Well, a vision is sufficient until it isn't. And I know that's a frustrating answer, because you want to know when your vision should evolve. You want to know when you should progress from one stage of the vortex to the next. You want to know when it's time to move to the next phase of the spiral. But these are natural and organic growth spirals. The answer to "When is it time?" is always

"When you are ready." Part of embracing the feminine, flow side of the spiral is accepting that there's no prescriptive answer and being able to tune into your own intuition to know when you're ready. No one can know when you're ready but you.

CHAPTER EIGHTEEN

Emotional Indicators

EMOTIONS ARE SO IMPORTANT TO HUMANS that we tend to use them as goals in and of themselves. If you ask people on the street, "What do you want out of life?" they're probably going to tell you that they want to be happy. They want the feeling. They might not use the word *happy* exactly. It may be some other word to describe how they want to feel. Danielle LaPorte built a whole system around answering the question "How do you want to feel?" and making people's core desired feelings be the objective of their life's work. Instead of accomplishment-based goals, she recommends pursuing emotion-based goals.

That's certainly an interesting approach, and quite different from a traditional approach to goal setting. For a time, I appreciated feelings as goals as a refreshing alternative to accomplishment-based goals. Asking the question "How do I want to feel?" totally revolutionized the way I thought about what I wanted and the way I made decisions about actions to take, what to do, with whom to engage, and how. It was a powerful shift for me.

But as I moved forward on my personal development journey, I realized that asking about feelings and emotions and using those as goals is a little bit misplaced. Even the core desired feelings of

LaPorte's work are really more along the lines of core values, which are slightly different from emotions. Feelings are a helpful but simplified way of communicating the idea of values. And what really revolutionized my way of thinking about goals, objectives, and visions was framing it around values, as opposed to either accomplishments or emotions.

As I dug deeper around vision crafting and then setting corresponding goals that are sustainable, are long lasting, and have the best chance of guaranteeing satisfaction at the end of the day, the question "Who do you want to *be*?" seemed the best start. This is why *being* is half of the foundation of your comprehensive vision. Living in service to your values certainly improves your emotions, while being out of alignment with values has a negative effect. But I've found that in order to create those sustainable and satisfying visions and goals, the best approach is to take emotions right out of it.

Emotions are responses to situations around you, such as perceived threats or opportunities. It's hard to control your emotions. You can do it to a certain extent, but it takes a whole lot of internal energy to exercise that kind of control.

Emotions are, in fact, indicators. They're gauges. Emotions are there to tell you when something is aligned with your core values and your outlooks and your true desires or not.

When you're flying an airplane, there are gauges that indicate all sorts of information about the state of the plane and the flight. But you can't fly an airplane using the gauges themselves—you need to have your hands or feet on the controls. You wouldn't say "I'd like to adjust my altitude, so I'm going to change the altimeter, here." No! That would just be silly. If you want to change altitude, you push or pull on the stick, and as your altitude changes as a result of that action, your altimeter reflects the change.

Similarly, if emotions are indicators or gauges, you wouldn't say "I'm going to adjust my happiness level." You are going to take actions that change your situation, and your happiness level will reflect the change.

In her book, *The New Feminine Brain*, Dr. Mona Lisa Schulz goes into this idea in great detail. Dr. Schulz asserts that our wide-ranging spectrum of emotions is actually made up of a core of five basic emotions: joy, sadness, anger, fear, and shame. (It sounds like the cast of the movie *Inside Out*, probably because the film was based on psychological research.) Joy is generally considered to be a positive emotion. The others—fear, sadness, anger, and shame—are perceived as negative. All other emotions are combinations of various concentrations of these basic emotions.

Schulz's research supports this idea of emotional indicators. She observes that, as a culture, we tend to vilify what are perceived as negative emotions. We believe that they're bad, and we want to get rid of them, or avoid them. If they show up for us, we want to fix them as quickly as possible and move back into a more positive emotional state.

But if you accept that emotions are indicators, those so-called negative emotions, which are part of the absolutely normal range of human emotional experience, are actually trying to tell you something. They're trying to get you to do the deep work and make the changes required to put you on a more sustainably joyful path.

The cultural impetus to fix these negative emotions as quickly as possible drives people to numbing behaviors and stopgaps that aren't effective in the long term. People turn to drugs and alcohol, emotionally eat, emotionally shop—all in pursuit of fixing the negative feelings as quickly as possible.

In reality, when you have those negative emotions, especially on a consistent basis, you need to identify what specific situation you're responding to. Then ask if it's something that needs to be worked on or if it's something that will pass. If it's part of a systemic misalignment with your eventual goals and vision, that's when it's time to do the deeper work to make change.

What does this all have to do with putting the spiral into practice? You already know that the spiral happens whether you like it or not. Sometimes the spiral can pull you kicking and screaming along with it. But other times, you know you're ready to transition into the next phase of the spiral. Knowing that you'll come around again, you can make that shift and leverage the gifts of that part of the spiral while leaving behind the gifts of the previous part of the spiral. You'll be able to leverage them even more perfectly the next revolution.

I find that when I'm acting in alignment with the phase of the spiral I'm in, I naturally experience positive emotions. Happy emotions come with productivity, when everything is humming along. Things are clicking together. It feels as if there's a certain synchronicity about what I do because I'm not trying to fight against the tide. I'm not trying to swim upstream. Because I'm acting in alignment with where I'm naturally being pulled, it's easy to find these positive emotions.

If you are falling victim to the belief that the grass is always greener on the other side of the spiral, and you're feeling uncomfortable or even resentful about where you are, then your mode of operating is misaligned with where you are right now in the cycle. As you fight against the natural flow of your own creative cycle, perhaps wishing you were in a different phase, you may experience a sense of envy of another phase, or even a sense of anger at yourself that you can't access the skills from the other side.

If you're experiencing negative emotions while spiraling, first ask yourself, "What phase of the spiral am I in? Are the tools I'm wishing for part of a different phase? How can I recognize the gifts of the spiral phase that I'm in now?"

Another reason you might experience negative emotions during the spiral is that it's time to move on to the next phase. If you've been resting, retreating, taking a break, and evaluating, and all of a sudden you start to feel bored and restless, it may be time to welcome Inspiration. That boredom, that itch to create momentum, means it's time to move forward into the next part of the spiral. Those feelings are indicators that it's time to adjust.

Similarly, if you have been taking a ton of action, stepping into the spotlight, and doing the work of Investigation, and you start to feel tired and irritable (as if all you want to do is put on fuzzy socks, crawl in a cave, and read a novel), it might be time to move toward rest, relaxation, and Introspection.

If you've been in a time of Inspiration where the ideas are coming at you in rapid-fire succession, and you're feeling a pull to focus, it's time to move into the Implementation. It's time to put pen to paper, play around with raw material, and create your vision.

You can see how experiencing what you might perceive as a negative emotion—boredom, exhaustion, irritability, nervousness, overwhelm—can simply indicate that it's time to do the next thing, to move on. These so-called negative emotions don't mean that you're doing something wrong. Your mind (or maybe your muse) is just trying to wave a flag at you to indicate that you're ready for the next phase.

The next time you're feeling one of those negative emotions, take the time to step back and say, "What am I ready for that I wasn't ready for last week? Am I ready to move on? Am I ready to let go of this thing I was doing, the phase I was in? Am I ready to transition into this next phase, to take it up a notch?"

That's what emotional indicators are for. They are not feelings that need to be numbed immediately by whatever (temporary, possibly harmful) means necessary. They are indicators that something is ready to change. Sometimes, it means that something fundamentally out of alignment needs to be fixed, and it requires deep inner work. But other times it doesn't mean that anything needs to be fixed or that anything was wrong in the first place. It simply means you are moving forward through the natural ebb and flow of the cycles, and you are ready. It's time to make the transition. Please don't ignore the signs that are given to you as a gift of the natural process. Listen to them.

This is the answer to the question from the last chapter. This is how you know when it's time to evolve the vision to something more specific. This is when you know that you're moving to the next stage of the vortex. This is how you know when it's time to move to the next phase of the spiral.

If you feel happy, confident, and motivated, you're in the right place. If you feel a little nervous because you're about to step across the void into something new and exciting, like you're about to jump out of an airplane and go skydiving for the first time, then you're in the right place.

If you feel terrified, nauseated, and bored, then something is out of alignment. If you are losing sleep or your relationship is starting to suffer, then something is out of alignment. You're not in the right place, your vision isn't serving you, and you need something else before you can move forward. Time to try something new.

How do you know what to change if your emotional indicators are telling you that something is out of alignment? Well, there's no great answer for that.

In the Disney Pixar film *Inside Out*, basic emotional responses are represented as characters in a young human mind. When she's a baby, the control panel in her mind has a single button on it. Emotional responses are very simple. As a child, the control panel has grown, and there are a few more dials and knobs to turn. As she ages into adolescence, her inner control panel gets reinstalled so that it's huge, with lots of complex-looking equipment.

You have lots of inner dials and knobs to turn, lots of different buttons to push and levers to throw within yourself. It's up to you to figure out how you are going to respond to your emotional indicators, which are basic primal responses. Which knobs can you turn or what levers can you throw to change things up? As you grow, your control panel gets more complex, but you also develop more self-awareness to help you figure out which changes to make to shift your emotional responses.

On the other hand, the presence of discomfort or other negative emotions doesn't always indicate something wildly out of whack. Deep down inside me I've known that I was supposed to write this book. The process of writing it has been rather difficult for me—I have trouble prioritizing it in my life and work, I suffer from various writer's blocks, and I find it hard to focus. But I know that writing this book is a good thing, and I want to do it. In this case, the discomfort is mostly coming from my own inner Resistance, my primal voice of fear that's afraid of being eaten by a saber-toothed tiger if I step out and allow myself to be seen.

How do I know that this is the source of my discomfort? My inner voice, my inner knowing deep inside my heart tells me it's true.

Throughout this writing process, I've tried to be mindful of the subtle shifts in discomfort that indicate when it's time to take a break or stop banging my head against a particular passage and get it over to my editor for feedback. I don't want to dig my heels in when I'm actually supposed to move on. But my general emotional frustration doesn't mean that I shouldn't be writing the book. It doesn't mean that the topic isn't important and that the words don't need to be said. It means I'm doing the hard work of birthing a new idea into the world.

Somewhere inside you, you know the answer. You know if the problem is that the vision is not specific enough. You know if the problem is that you just need to put your head down and push through it. You know if you need to take a break. You know if you need to focus on one particular thing or entertain new and diverse ideas. You know if it's time to move forward in the spiral. The voice of your intuition is going to help you identify the core issue that's upsetting your emotional indicators. Listen to it, and then make a plan to move forward.

This is part of your own personal Mystery. This is the beauty of the process. You get to learn this about yourself and figure out how to harness it. This is why entrepreneurship is the best personal development program you'll ever embark on. You have to know yourself well, deeply, and thoroughly. You have to think of yourself as a complex, whole person. And you get to decide if you're going to be held back or propelled forward when your emotional indicators are out of whack.

CHAPTER NINETEEN

Your Toolbox

WHAT WE'RE GOING TO TALK ABOUT NEXT is a very practical application of the spiral and the dichotomies it embodies, along with the vortex stages of the Creator's Journey. When we talked about spiral theory, we talked about engaging with all the different portions of the cycles. We also talked about splitting the spiral into halves and looking at it in terms of dichotomy—not exclusive dichotomy that allows you to say, "I am this and not that," but dichotomy that allows you to simplify how you think about the spiral.

The focus is on one of those simplifying dichotomies: structure and flow. Those two qualities could also be represented fairly well by saying masculine and feminine or yang and yin, or however it makes most sense to you.

How can you use practical tools of structure to give you that sense of reliability and security that you need to buy down that internal level of risk and to calm your internal fears so you feel that what you're moving toward is sustainable? How can you use the tools of flow, on the other side, to allow the freedom for inspiration and the flexibility for growth?

The thing about structure and flow is that one enables the other. The structure provides the framework. It provides the big, empty space in which flow and magic can happen. Without flow happening, there's no reason for structure to exist. It is the *raison d'être* of the structure in the first place. And even beyond that, flow enables the structure to grow in the direction you want so that the structure ends up being a living, breathing organism and not a static or stagnant entity.

You've already seen that you don't have one or the other of any of these seemingly opposing forces. You have both. You have a microcosm of the universe deep inside you.

That doesn't mean you don't have a preferred way of working, a natural tendency that you drift toward when all else is equal. But it also doesn't mean that the opposite way of working isn't accessible to you.

It's like having two hands (which you most likely do). You have a dominant hand—one that's particularly dexterous at certain activities—that you rely on. But do you go through life using only one hand? Would you not notice if your second hand were tied behind your back? Imagine what it would be like if you said, "I'm right handed, not left handed," and then you proceeded with "Since I'm right handed, I should use only my right hand, and I should give up my left hand. I won't use it since it must be useless. Its strengths aren't accessible to me." Sounds ridiculous, right?

Not only is your nondominant hand useful to assist your dominant hand in lifting heavy packages, clapping, or giving hugs, your nondominant hand may have strengths of its own.

When my children were babies, I would carry them on my left hip. They were wrapped up in and supported by my left arm—my nondominant arm. This freed my dominant right hand to do dexterous detail work such as adding ingredients to a pot, banging out an email on my laptop keyboard, or starting the washing machine. During this time, the muscles on my left side got incredibly strong because they were my go-to heavy lifters, my go-to precious-cargo holders. My nondominant muscles became strong—much stronger, in fact, than my dominant-side muscles. I needed my nondominant hand for a specific task for which it was better equipped than my dominant hand.

And so it is with these psychological, emotional, and spiritual dichotomies. Saying "I'm left brained, logical, and analytical; I'm not right brained, creative, and artistic" is the equivalent of tying one hand behind your back. Sure, your brain has a dominant state, a preferred way of working. But that doesn't mean you've got nothing on the other side. And it doesn't mean that your nondominant way of working doesn't have its own strengths, skills, and advantages.

Your nondominant strengths are as accessible to you as your nondominant hand. They're with you all the time, waiting to be called on. They're also very like a muscle—they get stronger when you use them.

So, when will you stop going through life with one side of your brain tied behind your back?

Although both sides of your brain, your psyche, and your personality have their own individual strengths and can be engaged independently, it's so crucial to remember that they can be used together. Your hands can be used independently or together. So can your strengths, opposite though they may seem. In fact, just as you're much stronger when you use both of your hands, you're much stronger, more adaptable, and more powerful when you use your entire suite of tools.

Structure and flow, then, become tools in your toolbox for growing your business and for life in general.

Before we take a look at integrating these fantastic strengths, let's take a look at the actual tools you have when you engage your capacity for structure and flow. You may be surprised to find that you've already got tools you use every day on your nondominant side, but you didn't give them the credit they deserved as being useful toward the very specific purpose of building your business and achieving your dreams. But I assure you they're there, waiting for you to acknowledge their value, waiting to be harnessed and put to work to make you more effective and efficient. And to make you happier while you do it.

It's time to untie your hands and step into the strength you've always had latent within you.

Structure

Structure is important in your business because it holds the space for flow, which is where the magic happens. Structure enables flow. Structure releases your brain from the mundane and allows you to elevate your thoughts to something much larger than yourself.

Structure provides:

- **Focus**. When lots of things are calling your name, but you need to see something through to get to a sense of accomplishment, structure is there to give you the whys and hows of getting it done.

- **Efficiency**. Structure stops you from having to reinvent the wheel every time. It sets up consistent practices that you don't even have to think about using so that you can use your creative energy on generating new things that really matter for you and your clients.

- **Guidance**. The creative journey can feel chaotic and aimless at times. It's easy to feel lost and then let your emotional reaction induce panic and stress. The structure is there to bring you back to your sense of purpose and priority, and sometimes to remind you that you do actually know what you are doing.

- **Reliability**. A structure helps you deliver consistent results every time. This has far-reaching impacts for you (less stress and more confidence) and for your clients (greater confidence that you'll be able to solve their problem and a more appealing experience).

- **Scalability**. We all have the dream of moving from dollars-for-hours into exponential growth and/or passive income. Structure helps you get your business to a place where the systematization required for scalability is possible, as well as achieve it with the aforementioned reliability.

- **(Safe) Space**. The literal definition of *structure* is the creation of space. Your bones create space for your internal organs. The tent poles of a circus tent create the container for the greatest show on Earth. The struts and skin of a spacecraft create a space that can sustain life in the middle of an uninhabitable void. And the structure of your business creates the space for you to make your magic. Without structure, there is no space.

Here are some tools of structure that you have available in your toolbox:

- Project plans and execution

- Rituals

- Systems

- Branding and messaging

- Data and analysis

Project Plans and Execution

The purpose of your vision is to provide you with a destination to aim toward. We know the destination may change, but in order to start moving, you have to head out in a direction.

The vision gives you that.

Project plans and execution are the road map for getting to the vision. Again, you aren't going for something so prescriptive that you turn your brain off and ignore contextual signs and signals coming in through your five senses along the way. But it's helpful to have guidelines. The project plans are there so that when you feel a bit lost, you have something to check in with to say, "Hey, I remember where I said I was going. Here's what I can do next to move me in that direction."

Project plans can take so many forms and exist at so many levels of specificity that I could write a whole book on the subject. But here are a few ways you can keep a road map of plans for yourself so you can keep moving toward your vision.

Spiral Road Map. In this book, you've seen the power of design spirals for iteratively developing what you want to call into existence. And the design spirals provide a gentle structure themselves for shifting back and forth between structured work and flow, between yin and yang, between masculine and feminine energy.

Each spiral should advance you through the spiral vortex, and it takes one trip or more around the spiral per stage of the vortex—the Mystery spiral(s), the Heuristic spiral(s), and the Algorithm spiral(s). So, here we take that concept and make it practical. For each project that you work on, take the time to map out what each spiral looks like, how it's scoped, and perhaps most importantly, how it's going to help you move through the spiral vortex.

This project planning format isn't arbitrarily tied to dates (unless you want it to be and have a particular launch date in mind), and it's something that grows organically out of the simple act of walking the creative path. If you get off of this road map and decide to chase inspiration elsewhere, it's relatively easy to get right back on because you have a concept of where you were at the time and where you were headed. In fact, I'd say that this kind of road map lends itself quite well to those sorts of creative rabbit trails and provides you with enough structure to find the trail again.

A Menu of Tasks. A menu of items is a fantastic alternative to traditional, rigid plans. Since you are only assigning due dates to items that really need them as we discussed above, a menu helps you keep track of what's on your list. A menu of tasks allows you to choose what you feel like doing and adapt your plan to the time allowed.

I'm an extremely busy person, pulled in a thousand directions at once—the kids, the house, the business, homeschool lesson planning, calendar coordination with my husband, social interaction, meal planning, the occasional vehicle-breakdown crisis, shopping, eating more vegetables, responding to creative inspiration, self-care, getting to bed at a less-than-obscene hour—well, you see how it is. I'm betting you have a similar set of demands on your time and attention. It's so hard in this environment to block time for tasks that don't have an absolute deadline on them. So, if you keep a menu of tasks at the ready—things that you need or want to get done—in those magical thin slices of time that open up unexpectedly, you won't spend the whole thin slice of time trying to figure out what you were supposed to be doing with it. You refer to your menu, tune into what's the most important, most effective, and (or) most enjoyable way to use your thin slice of time, and you get to it. Nothing supports action-taking quite like reminding yourself how you can take action.

This form of structure, you'll notice, also supports a certain sense of flow. There is nothing prescriptive about what you *have* to do at any given time. Instead, you get to decide. You get to feel into it. You get to follow the inspiration and motivation that strike you.

A word about unpleasant tasks. Yes, there are things that need to get done that aren't always enjoyable. Your intuition will not always lovingly purr its desire to call the credit card company about that weird charge you saw come through. So, think not only about how much joy, pleasure, and freedom each task brings you in the moment of doing it, but also about the level of joy, pleasure, and freedom you'll receive once the unpleasant task is done. Also, you are a grown-up. I figure that by now you know when you need to just suck it up and do the hard stuff.

Rituals

Humans are creatures of ritual. Ritual, to me, even though I have it categorized here under "structure," is one of the hallmarks of the integration of structure and flow.

Ritual is structured by definition. It's something that's done the same way—or mostly the same way—every time. But ritual, unlike a process or a system or a checklist that's mechanistic and robotic in nature, is organic and natural.

Plants and humans grow according to the road map of our DNA. The DNA is interpreted so that a type of organism is built the same way every single time. This doesn't preclude mutation or adaptation to the surrounding environment that alters the road map, the construction of the organism, and the DNA itself (which is how we get evolutionary development). So it is with ritual.

Ritual provides the vehicle to interpret an event the same way every single time. But that doesn't preclude adaptation to the specific circumstances surrounding the event and evolutionary growth of the ritual (resulting in evolutionary growth of the human or group of humans).

The word *ritual* sounds as if it's related to religion because it contains spiritual and emotional connections. The connection of a process to emotion and to the higher good is what gives the ritual its power. A ritual without emotion or spirit is just another mechanistic process. Infusing your processes with emotion, with spirit, and with a sense of awe and holiness increases their sticking power and their magnetism to keep you engaging with them.

Example: Weekly planning of your business rhythms can be a box to check—a totally rote procedure of reviewing your appointments and updating your to-do list. But turning it into a ritual means acknowledging that planning is sacred self-care. It honors your individual needs and it honors the work you're doing in the world. It's a way to connect with yourself as you reflect on how you want to *be* and what you want to *do* on a granular, day-to-day basis that ties back into the overarching vision for your life and work.

Ritual is a structure that also directly holds space for a sense of flow by creating a time of rest and reflection. Your time in ritual is the empty space you need to take a moment, celebrate your wins, mourn your losses, and reflect on the way in which what you're working on fits into the bigger picture. A planning ritual also allows you to create some empty spaces throughout the week or month to have more creative or meditative time—the empty space you need to be open to receiving, open to inspiration and flow.

Systems

Systems take the guesswork out of the simple processes you do all the time in your business. If you don't have to reinvent the wheel every single time you do something, you free up your precious brain space to do more of what you love to do. To do more of your genius work. To do more of what you are called to do on this planet.

Systems can take several forms. First they can accomplish mundane tasks, taking innovative function out of something that doesn't actually need innovation. This can look like a work flow for onboarding a client. This can look like your procedure for posting a piece of content after you've produced it. In the latter example, a standard flow may look something like this:

1. Do a live broadcast on social media to produce new content from an idea.

2. Transcribe your video broadcast to text.

3. Take out the weird artifacts and tics of speech, and shore up the logical flow so that it becomes a blog post.

4. Pull out a few juicy quotes and make pretty social media images.

5. Schedule the blog and the social media images to post on social media channels.

6. Write up and schedule an email blast to go out to your list about the new content.

All it takes is a simple jotting down of this standard process to remind you that you know how to do this, that you do it the same way every time, and that you shouldn't have to think about how to do it the next time.

At the minimum, this little procedure becomes something you could execute easily in your sleep. And that's not just a figure of speech. In order to create original content and be creative, I have to be in the zone. I have to be fresh and rested. To write this book, I've been setting my alarm for zero-dark-thirty to get up a mere half hour before my early-bird children sound their cock-a-doodle-doo all over my house. I need to do this to do the creative work of writing. If I wait until my primary work time, which is after they go to bed at night, I am so depleted that I just stare at the blank page while nothing comes until it's too late to say that I'm going to bed at a decent time. Then, I feel guilty about everything I didn't do.

The point is, these systems and processes are Algorithms that can be done in that state of creative depletion because the system takes the creativity out of it. And in this case, that's a good thing. This means you get to use that time functionally when you would otherwise be staring at the wall, and you can save those precious moments of freshness at 5:30 a.m. for doing the creative work you really need to do.

The other side of systems is that they provide you with consistent and reliable results for your clients or for whatever creative work you do. There's certainly power in simply listening to what the problem is and then digging deep to create custom solutions every time. But the key to scalability for your business is to systematize what you do for people. This starts to happen in the Heuristic stage of the vortex, but at its core, a system that produces consistently predictable results for your clients is, by definition, an Algorithm.

Will every single solution involve an Algorithm? Will a solution be completely encompassed by an Algorithm so that you don't need to customize or tailor it? Maybe not. And that can be a good thing, because that's how you start to create new solutions. But having these go-to tools or processes helps you with that scalability and frees up your creative function. It also gives your client a sense of structure. And structure at healthy levels provides comfort and security.

By using proven, regular systems that feel natural to you and aren't strewn with the mental detritus of "figuring it out" all the time, you pass on that feeling of *gemütlichkeit* (pleasant warmth that comes from feeling they're in the right place) to your clients.

What are some other systems? They might look like

- Intake forms

- Courses

- Assessments

- Worksheets

- Events with a standard flow or agenda

- Exercises

- Recipes

- Formulas

- Apps or other software

Your clients will thank you, and you'll feel stronger and more consistent. Clarity in articulation falls out of this. You get to be strong and specific about what you do to help people and how you make a difference in the world.

Branding and Messaging

No part of business structure offers more consternation and requires an unreasonably high percentage of time than branding. For some reason, branding is the structural element that has entrepreneurs convinced that if they just have it nailed down, everything else in the business will fall into place. So, we obsess over colors, fonts, logos, and web design. We endlessly tweak the Home and About pages in the hopes that the one right person will catch a glimpse of the magic behind our work through the words and pixels. It's like casting spells, and we sit there muttering incantations when we could be out doing the work.

Branding is an important piece of the business structure. It takes the guesswork out of how you show up in the world and speak to mass audiences. You don't have to use precious brainpower to select your fonts or colors, or even some of your subject matter. All of those details are already laid out for you, and they provide the context for new innovation to come and fit into what you've already said. You don't have to waste precious brainpower selecting these elements every time, but you still end up with visual consistency. Visual consistency for your reader/client/web passerby means they have an easier time processing the new information; it appears consistent, congruent, and in context.

Where do we go so wrong? Where do we get the idea that if we just work this bit out, our business will be successful? I can suggest a few reasons for this. We know that a picture is worth a thousand words and that visual elements are a critical part of user experience. We know this from our own experience as users. We understand the impact of a solid brand and an online experience. And it seems easier (and more fun) to work on these shiny bits and bobs of garnish in the forefront rather than on the meat and potatoes of what you offer, even though it's ultimately the meat and potatoes that form the backbone of your revenue. Ultimately, the garnish isn't actually important when compared to the taste and nutritional profile of the meal itself.

I think it definitely helps to view the visual branding and messaging components as part of the business structure—touch points to go to when you feel lost in order to be found again. Guideposts to keep you on track. And grease for the wheels of your own business efficiency so you can dedicate your brainpower to something way more important and effective. In the case of branding, the structure also shows up directly for customers. When branding gives your content a sense of predictability and context, it's easier for them to take in because they don't have to spend their precious brainpower trying to cram whatever is new or "out of family" into the context of your business for you. Instead, they can focus on integrating the content, seeing how it (and, therefore, you) can help them solve their problems. They can have an authentic emotional response to the actual content and solutions, not to the user experience.

A good brand will kickstart the customers' emotional experience and start to form the attachment to you and your work. But the attachment and the emotional connection won't last long unless there are good bones beneath the shiny exterior. So, yes, use the branding for the ease of consistency and the initial emotional impact. But don't forget that it's only the beginning of what your client truly needs to do with your business in order to build trust, be fully engaged, and press the "Go" button on your products or services.

Data and Analysis

There's something about data analysis that makes people either love it or hate it. As for me, I'm a numbers nerd, so I love data. I could swim in data. I could subsist on a healthy diet of data. I used to keep every aspect of my life in spreadsheets, from fitness tracking and meal planning to frequent-flyer mile earnings. (Then I had children, which is a whole other story.) Suffice it to say, if there's a way to summarize and interpret data, I'm usually all over it.

But I recognize that not everyone is like me. In fact, if you're not like me, I've found that most likely you're the polar opposite of me, and the thought of data analysis nearly causes you to break out in hives.

My hope is that if you're allergic to data and analysis, I'm going to give you some ideas about how they can help you without being so scary, boring, or difficult. (If you are my nerd-buddy and adore data, then I doubt I have to convince you.)

In a conference room where I used to work operating interplanetary spacecraft, there was a sign posted that read "In God We Trust. All others bring data." In the engineering world, data is the ultimate arbiter of decision-making. (Well, it should be, anyway. Interestingly, engineers are humans too, and they make decisions based on emotions or intuition far more often than they like to admit. But I digress.)

I'm not out to make data the be-all and end-all of our creative process or strategic decision-making, but it is a tool in the toolbox. Data allows us to assess how things are going so that we can make decisions about how to move forward. It grounds the decisions made by our intuition in fact—in rationality.

What types of data you collect very much depend on the creative project you've got going and what problem you are trying to solve. In some cases, data is quantitative and objective: how much money is spent, lost, or saved; how fast a task is completed; how much fat is lost or muscle gained. In other cases, data is qualitative and subjective: customer satisfaction ratings, user experience ratings, emotional outcomes. Don't fool yourself into thinking that if a metric isn't totally quantifiable, it's useless. Any way you can measure your progress, your impact, your engagement, or your success tells you something.

At the same time, it's important to understand the limitations of what data can tell you. All data is subject to interpretation, so all data must be taken with a grain of salt. One result of the Heisenberg Uncertainty Principle (one of my favorite physics concepts) is that just by attempting to measure a property of a particle (in this case, position or velocity), you necessarily disturb it so that the measurement is inaccurate. Even the highest science acknowledges that uncertainty exists and that measurement is hard.

Don't let that discourage you from taking data. In fact, it should encourage you to know that all you are looking for is guidance—a milestone that shows you you're headed in the direction you want to be.

Ask yourself:

- What would signal to me that what I'm doing is working?

- What would signal to me that what I'm doing is *not* working?

- What do I need to know to make this better in the next spiral?

Look for ways to measure these concepts.

Once you have your data, you are going to want to analyze it. Just having the data sitting there isn't going to help you. You have to actually look at it, understand it, interpret it, and figure out what it's trying to tell you.

Analysis is made up of two main processes: decomposition and synthesis. In decomposition you can look at individual questions or individual case studies to answer specific, detailed questions. This gives you a perspective on the breadth of what you're doing and all of the unique permutations. In synthesis, you draw all the data together and look for threads, themes, or stories. This gives you a general consensus around the efficacy of what you are doing.

You can start to play with metrics such as average response, standard deviation, and maximum or minimum responses. These metrics help you characterize the general experience of your creation, and they help answer those fundamental questions about whether you're on the right track. They can also help you identify outliers in the data, so that you don't feel the need to make wholesale changes on the experiences of a tiny subset of your clientele, unless you really want to. No single metric is going to give you the whole picture, but they all come together (in synthesis) to help you understand yourself and your creative work.

Ultimately you want to ask, "What story is the data telling?" Looking for the narrative embedded in the data really brings it to life. Data by itself is dry, flat, and practically meaningless. It's the narrative crafted around the data about the *why* and the *how* of the way things are happening that make data so powerful. It's analysis that draws out this narrative.

You'll use your data and analysis toolbox the most in the Investigation phase of the spiral, but data and analysis are there for you any time you need to ground a hunch in reality.

Flow

Flow is important in your business because it's where the magic happens. Flow enables creativity and inspiration. Flow is your original thought. It's how you, as a single individual in the scope of human history, are able to impact this world.

When I sat down to write this section of this book, I was frustrated that there just wasn't that much to say about flow, although I had all sorts of commentary on structure. But I realized that this is just the point, isn't it? In flow is where we listen. In flow is where we receive. It's in the empty space of flow that we're inspired to innovation, to new ideas. If we find ourselves talking and *doing* so much, we must ask ourselves if we are really allowing flow to work its magic.

How does flow show up in your business, in your life, in your world? Look for it in the grace of empty space.

Here are some tools of flow that you have available in your toolbox:

- Meditation

- Creative outlets/play

- Creative empty space

- Networking and relationship building

- Self-care

- Reflection and reevaluation

Meditation

The best way to create empty space is to be in the habit of creating empty space. This can be difficult in a world where there are so many demands on our time and such a premium placed on accomplishment. The way you get good at creating empty space is to make empty space a habit.

Meditation is a way to do that.

A meditation practice gives your brain a break. By doing this on a regular basis (daily is ideal), you are creating a rhythm of rest for your brain. Not only is it healthy to create that space for yourself on a regular basis, but being in the habit of meditation can help you create empty space whenever you need it, even if it's not your usual practice time.

Meditation can take different forms. You can simply focus on your breathing. You can give attention to each part of your body. You can chant a mantra, or you can be silent. You can be sitting or walking. You can have silence, listen to music, or listen to a speaking voice prompting you what to focus on.

In the Resources section, you'll find a few for starting a meditation practice. But without getting all fancy, the point is that it's good to prioritize (and not avoid) empty space.

Silence the voice that's telling you you're lazy if you're not in motion, and be present in the moment.

Creative Outlets and Play

Similar to allowing habitual empty space, your brain needs to be in the habit of playing around. It's really hard to be creative on demand when you aren't used to freeing your mind and letting it run wild with possibilities, without regard for probabilities. So, play is something that you can practice. The great thing about practicing play is that it's not a chore—it's totally fun! If it's not fun when you're practicing play, you're doing it wrong. Julia Cameron, author of *The Artist's Way*, has some fantastic suggestions for how to play deliberately in order to foster your sense of creative intuition. My favorites of her methods are the artist's date and morning pages.

An artist's date is a time that you set aside once a week or once a month to do something creative or artistic, or to simply feed your creative soul. It doesn't have to be related to your business or to productivity (some would argue that it *shouldn't* be). It's just an avenue for you to try new things, to experience and enjoy beauty, and to connect with a part of yourself that's easy to forget when you are busy busy busy. You could try something you've always wanted to do, like throw pottery on a wheel, take up martial arts, or go to one of those "canvas and cocktails" events. You could do something you used to do but don't have time for anymore, such as go to a choral singing event or take your journal into the woods to write some poetry. You could experience someone else's art at a gallery, concert, or performance. Anything that makes you feel more open, more appreciative of beauty, or more alive can be an artist's date.

The other practice from Julia Cameron is writing morning pages. Strictly speaking, these are three pages of longhand, written first thing in the morning before doing anything—yes, before checking your phone! (Can you handle it?) The idea is that writing morning pages gets the gunk out of your brain that's standing between you and your next creative breakthrough. It gives that gunk an outlet so that you can access the brilliant stuff that's underneath.

But morning pages can be used for all manner of things. They don't have to be observed in the strictest sense. Morning pages can be written or typed. They can be stream of consciousness, a response to a journal prompt, or intentional writing. For example, I find that my most potently creative time is first thing in the morning when I'm fresh and my brain is still untainted by social media or the crises of the day. That sacred half hour between when my feet hit the floor and when my kids descend is my most insightful time. That's the time when you'll find me pounding away at my keyboard, putting together books like this one. The benefit of doing this as a practice is to show up and do the work, which is what Steven Pressfield preaches in *The War of Art*. This is my time to show up every day and let the muses do as they will. I've done my part. It also makes me feel so productive. No matter what else happens during the day, I have a sense of productivity and accomplishment because I wrote something meaningful—before anyone else was awake.

A creative outlet doesn't have to be as structured (see what I did there?) as these artist- date and morning-page activities. At the heart of it, these creative expressions are rooted in being able to let yourself go and play. Play as if you were a kid again. Stop taking yourself and your creativity so dang seriously. Nothing feeds creativity the way play does. To experience this, all you have to do is spend time with a six-year-old who's into Lego, or a five-year-old who likes to draw. A practice of play is practicing the ability to let go and let whatever comes, come. The artist's date and the morning pages frameworks can help get you there if you have trouble with the letting go. But make no mistake, the letting go is the ultimate objective here.

Play is a crucial and powerful way to access your creative power. Play takes the pressure off because there is no expectation. There is no real objective other than having fun and seeing what's possible.

Sold on play? How do you go about it then? You think like a child does. Anything a child would be interested in spending time on is fair game. As the mother of a seven-year-old, a six-year-old, and a two-year-old, I'm well-equipped to give you a list of options if you don't have any. Here are a few suggestions:

- Build with Lego (other construction toys could be acceptable, I suppose, if you must)

- Draw with crayons

- Color (inside or outside the lines)

- Sculpt with beeswax clay

- Knit something

- Build forts out of couch cushions, dining room chairs, blankets, and/or tree branches

- Climb a tree

- Swing

- Take a bath and pretend you're a pirate (arrrrgh)

- Play "restaurant" or "store" by using your imagination

- Have a tea party (bonus if there are stuffed animals present)

- Play a board game that takes you to another world

- Go to your local children's museum for more ideas on imaginative and creative play

If you have trouble playing on your own at first (because you may have forgotten how to do it), I recommend hanging out with a kid or two who can show you how.

Let go of preconceived notions of how things are supposed to be, and let your mind run free. This is an exercise and a practice to help you disengage from having to be useful 100 percent of the time and to break you out of the rigidity of the structures that you allow to keep you locked in place, even if that's not what they were intended to do in the first place.

Play opens you up so that when it's time to apply that sense of possibility, freedom, and imagination to problems that really need solving, you can get there.

Creative Empty Space

In order to apply your creative skill to your work, there has to be open space to do it.

Do you find that your best business ideas come to you at the most inopportune times, like when you're in the shower, when you have your hands covered in raw meat while you mix up the meatloaf, or when you're sitting in rush-hour traffic? It's no accident that this is when ideas make themselves known. They show up at these seemingly awkward times when you have (perhaps inadvertently) created empty space in your mind. In fact, given all the activities and must-dos you try to shoehorn into your, the shower, the kitchen, and the car may be the only places in which you allow there to be empty space. So, your indomitable creative function doesn't hesitate. It will take what it can get.

You can certainly use these built-in empty spaces to exercise your creativity and to leverage the ideas that come, but it's also beneficial to set aside pockets of time for yourself in which nothing is expected except to turn your creative attention toward the work you really want to create in the world.

This is especially great for generating ideas around an already inspired idea. It's hard to get the lightning bolt of inspiration to strike at any given time, so you may find that the big ideas still come in the shower, the kitchen, or the car. But putting flesh on the bones of an idea and turning it into a real product or service that is useful and appealing to your clients requires deliberate, dedicated creative time to "play with your mental blocks," as my father-in-law would say.

It can be hard to create on demand, but that's why your previous practices of creating empty spaces and using those empty spaces to create will come in so handy. You've already experimented with meditation, with having artistic experiences, with dumping the ideas in your head on the page, with playing around. So now that you're in practice, if you create the space in which to do that stuff, you can point your creative energy in a desired direction (that is, your work) and focus that laser beam to create something amazing and specific.

How do you do this? My friend Annabel Melnyk, career and personal brand coach, calls this your "sacred container." She recommends creating a ritual around this creative time to set the space for this work and to signal your brain that it's time. You can light a candle or say a blessing. You can work with a specific notebook and pen or with a certain type of music playing in the background. And for goodness' sake, shut down social media and silence your phone! You create a sacred space that signals your creativity that it's safe to come out and play. That you won't be disturbed by minutiae. That it's dedicated time for dreaming about what could be rather than handling what is.

The most important part is that you not be interrupted for a bit. So if that means taking yourself out of your normal habitat of distractions or waking up before the kids do, then that's what it means.

Then, point your thoughts in the direction of what you want to create for your business and for your clients, and let what comes, come.

You know what direction that is because you have your big-picture vision creating a familiar framework in which to play.

Relationship Building and Networking

I've always been uncomfortable in networking situations. I'm a confident, outgoing sort of person (despite being an introvert), and it's always seemed so completely wrong that I'm paralyzed in fear by the concept of working a room.

I recently complained to my coach about this, seeing as how I have several conferences coming up soon. I hit a bit of a breakthrough during my outburst. I realized that what makes me so uncomfortable in those situations is a lack of structure. There don't seem to be rules. Or rather, there seems to be an unwritten set of rules that I am completely unaware of. As a person who tends toward structure rather than flow, this lack of rules bothers me greatly. It feels nigh unto impossible to figure out and makes me want to throw in the towel altogether.

Reframing relationship building and networking as elements of flow helps tremendously (although it doesn't entirely make me comfortable at a cocktail party). Relationships and collaboration are crucial parts of the feminine aspect, and they're also critically important in business. This is one place where rigid corporate America, with its love affair with robotic structure and repeatable process, understands the importance of the feminine aspect. Sayings such as "It's who you know" and "Deals are made on the golf course" demonstrate that it's commonly understood that relationships can help you move forward. It's important for strong masculine organizations to allow the relationships to be healthy, collaborative, and dynamic, and not become twisted into manipulative, fearful power struggles. I feel this within myself; my difficulty with building effective business relationships is rooted in a desire for control. It seems innocent enough that I like to control my environment and want to know and trust the rules that I interact with. But it's easy to see how that could grow and mutate into something ugly.

Relationship and collaboration in their purest forms are a release of individual control in exchange for the promotion of the collective. They can be unpredictable and surprising, but therein lies their beauty. In unpredictability, you will find a cauldron of creativity, with conditions that are perfect for innovation. And in this case, when you're not stuck behind your own desk, trapped in the confines of your own mind with your own personal demons, progress can be lightning fast when you tap the potential inside each participant of a team.

Sales is a relationship of collaboration. We help others co-create the result they're looking for in their lives. Sometimes this gets lost in the us-them construct of sales as a battle with the salesperson being the victor or not. But this is where we have lost our way. Even the most hardened business professional understands that sales is about relationships.

Instead of attempting to force our own wills in the sales conversation, what would happen if we fiercely nurtured our prospects, with unwavering attention to what they need and how they'd best be served? What if we dedicated our own unwavering commitment to truly hearing and supporting their dreams and desires, and throwing the log of our own creative energy on the fire of making those dreams reality? There would be magic, that's what.

As we allow the relationship to grow and develop organically, we are captured by the natural beauty inside it. We unwittingly create for ourselves this fertile greenhouse of possibility where new ideas can sprout and blossom. We open ourselves to new ideas that would have never come to us otherwise. We invite in the spark of inspiration, divinely provided by our fellow humans.

Understanding that relationship is flow and that collaboration is a feminine aspect is helpful to me to know how I should approach it. It's so much less about the rules of engagement and walking away with a series of objectives achieved. It's about being in flow with another human being, about allowing another person into your flow.

So how can we all do this better?

Forgetting about our agenda seems like the first way to allow relationships to fulfill their potential. We need to stop enforcing structure on something that's not intended to be structured.

True, deep, authentic listening is the key to embracing flow. In order to work in flow, we must quiet ourselves so that we can feel the flow happening. Individually, we do this through various forms of meditation to quiet the mind and listen to our inner knowing and to inspiration from the Divine Source. But here in the context of relationship, it's not so esoteric. We must quiet our own mind and our own need to express and be heard so that we can open ourselves to inspiration from the very corporeal source of *each other*.

Having done that—having quieted our own need for self-expression and opened ourselves to possibility and inspiration—we must come to know relationship and collaboration as courageous creative action, as a cauldron of creation and innovation. In this, we find the freedom to allow relationship to grow organically without enforcing predictability or rules that would necessarily restrict this potent, creative force.

Rest and Self-Care

Rest is something that's easy to accept as necessary. We all need to sleep every night. Oddly, however, rest is also something that's easy to use as a commodity, traded against a feeling of toughness and invincibility.

For some reason, even though we know we need it, self-care is viewed as a luxury, and rest is viewed as a weakness. When the masculine drive for accomplishment is at toxic levels, we brag about how long we were awake, about how many hours were spent slogging away without respite, and about how many small hours of sleep we've gotten for so many nights. It's as if, this is a badge of honor that proves just how worthy we are and just how significant our work is.

But there's no honor in abusing yourself with the deprivation of rest. It negatively affects your productivity. Ample rest not only helps you function at your best, it's required. Creativity is a high-energy sport. It requires freshness and recharge. If you want to be at your creative best, you must get sufficient rest to support and fuel the creative fire.

But if you struggle with allowing yourself to rest, repeat this as a mantra: if you want to be at your creative best, you must get sufficient rest.

We vilify and shun rest and self-care because it doesn't seem productive, and productivity is king. Even when we're able to justify it, it's done on the grounds that resting will make us more productive, which seems nearly as unhealthy.

Take the rest because you are human. Take the rest because you need it, and don't apologize. Take the rest because it supports you in your quest to live a happy, integrated life. The productivity and prolific creation that comes out of that is a bonus.

One way that toxic masculinity warps the concept of rest is that it glorifies waiting. Paying your dues. Standing by until someone else deems you worthy. When I worked in the corporate world, my most passionate goal was to be the chief systems architect for a large spacecraft program. I asked the technical leadership at my company about the path to get to this goal. I was told I needed to wait 10-15 years. Understanding how the corporate structure worked, this made a certain amount of sense. I lacked some experience and scar tissue, and I was willing to play by the rules in order to climb the fabled corporate ladder. So, I asked, "What should I do while I'm waiting? What experience should I seek? To whom should I apprentice?" The hostile, aggressive answer was "Do you want to be a senior fellow in systems architecture? You just have to wait." I was confident in my value as a team member in the present moment, not just after the magical 10-15 year timer went off. Although I may not have been ready for a senior-level position, the time in the interim should have been used for my highest good and for the good of the company.

Regardless of how much stillness is inside the rest, it's not an idle waiting for some external entity to deem you worthy. Periods of rest are periods of nurture, where you tend to the seeds that you've planted so that they will germinate, sprout, and take root.

(It turned out that "waiting" for 10-15 years was not a term I was willing to agree to. I stepped into the adventure of entrepreneurship so that I could be free of arbitrary structure and exercise some flow.)

Self-care is a similar story. We tend to feel guilty and defensive when we spend our precious resources of time and money on something as "frivolous" as self-care. We know the benefits of feeling good and well nurtured, but somehow, we need to remind ourselves loudly of those benefits every time. We treat self-care as if it were a reward or a treat instead of as a necessary part of our creative cycle. We deprive ourselves of the self-care that we need until we've sufficiently run ourselves into the ground to prove, yet again, that we are worthy.

We need that self-care to nurture and to tend the creative flame. It isn't a luxury; it's an investment in ourselves, our growth, and our forward progress.

Taken to the extreme, rest and self-care can look a lot like simple inactivity and waiting. And sometimes, that's what it needs to look like to serve us best in our cycles. But rest assured (ha—see what I did there?), the inactivity isn't simple and unlimited waiting. It's deliberate and necessary in the larger scope of the creative process.

Reflection and Reevaluation

Every so often, it's critically important to take a step back and take in the forest instead of just the trees. It's amazing how much we're drawn to say, "I don't have time for that! I can't stop now! I have to keep moving forward!" And then we wonder why burnout comes. Reflection and reevaluation (what I'm calling the new R&R) give us not only a chance to rest and switch gears but also a real opportunity for growth.

Within R&R, we plant the seeds of the innovative ideas yet to come. We're able to incorporate all of the learning that has come before and infuse it into our next step. We're growing and moving forward without banging our heads into the same old walls.

Ironically, while reflection and reevaluation seem like frivolous breaks in the action, it's in R&R that we can truly move forward, because we use the wisdom of experience to propel us.

So, what does R&R look like?

First, there is definitely an element of rest. Ongoing rest on the day-to-day level is part of self-care, for sure. But R&R rest means a real drawing back. Sometimes you need downtime and stillness for more than a few minutes or hours. Reflective rest has a longer duration and a greater depth than everyday rest.

Second, there is a turning inward. Instead of being out and active and visible, you're drawn inside. This allows you to check in with yourself. How do you feel? How are you doing? Are you on the right path? What needs to change to make this better for you, for the business, for your clients? It's definitely hard to check in with yourself when you're pushing forward all the time. Your body becomes a tool for the cause. In R&R, your body *is* the cause, and you can use your physically grounded intuition.

Third, there is a sense of curiosity, not only about the work itself but about the process of the work. Ask yourself the same questions: How is it going? What did I learn that I can apply going forward? And there's a sense of curiosity about the vision and the possibilities that lie ahead. Knowing what you know now, do you need to change where you are headed? You can miss possibilities if you keep your head down and your nose to the grindstone all the time. R&R is the chance you have to look up and see new paths emerging—ones you didn't even realize were there.

I was a person who thought I knew the path from the beginning. Do you remember Harold and the Purple Crayon from the beginning of this book? That was me! I drew myself a long, straight path so I didn't get lost, and I set out upon it. I thought that was the best way to achieve my goals—with focus and nothing but focus.

When I was 12 years old, I fell in love with space exploration. I decided that I was destined to be an astronaut and fly in space. But this was no ordinary childhood astronaut aspiration. No. For the next 15 years, every decision I made in my career, in my life's work, was to move toward that goal. I never really paused to look up from it. In my mind, there was one way to make a goal as big and as audacious as this one reality: to never stop driving toward it.

When I was 27 years old, having worked in Houston directly with astronauts, I found that the work wasn't totally aligned with my gifts, skills, and even more shockingly, my desires for the rest of my life. I put the astronaut application aside. But even then, I didn't stop and say, "Hey, it seems like what I want has changed. Maybe I should take a moment to really dig into what that change means for me." Instead, I pressed on along a path very much adjacent to the one I'd already been on. I focused all of my heart and intention on spacecraft architecture and design.

Because I hadn't truly stepped back to examine where I should go next, I struggled quite a bit in my career over the next few years. I banged my head against the internal walls of my unidentified desires and against the external walls of a corporate structure that I was attempting to navigate on my own terms, but without a compass or map.

It was having my first two children that caused me to stop for a second and think about where I was headed. And not in the "I have children now and all my priorities are different" sort of way. No, it was simply that maternity leave created the pause I needed to step back and say, "Wow, I made some big changes in my life vision in the past few years, and I never even stopped to ask myself if what I want has changed based on the person I've been becoming in the past 20 years, given all the things I've learned about the world and about myself."

What I found when I allowed myself the space and grace to reflect was that along the way, I'd developed a whole different set of skills that I wanted to utilize. I'd developed a whole different set of possibilities that seemed exciting to me. And the dreams that I'd previously been chasing so hard without looking up had become limiting beliefs. The concept that I was meant to make a difference in the world of space exploration was actually holding me back from exercising my potential.

And this period of R&R—which was really hard because I wasn't used to taking such a marked break and questioning everything— led me to the high-touch, high-impact profession of coaching and an architectural mind-set around business building. This latter piece rather shocked me when I stepped into it because I had beaten myself up so badly about stepping away from the dream that I "should" have been focused on. However, it turned out that as an entrepreneur and coach, I was using the same types of skills—albeit enhanced by new ones—to do something different, exciting, and powerful.

So, my questions for you are: Where in your world have you been assuming that you know all the answers? Where have you been assuming that the answers are the same as they've always been? Is it time to take a step back and explore those areas with fresh eyes? Allow yourself to pause, to have the gift of empty space to ask these questions. They're the key to unlocking the path forward.

PART V: THE END

CHAPTER TWENTY

Integration

THE GOLDEN GATE BRIDGE SITS WHERE THE PACIFIC OCEAN meets the San Francisco Bay, two separate but joined bodies of water. The waters mix. There's no wall that says that the ocean water can't come into the bay, and there's no wall that says the bay can't flow into the ocean. Indeed, ships and sea life cross back and forth all the time. There's no wall, but there's still an edge. There are thermoclines of temperature and environment. There's a mixture of fresh and salt water with named zones of salinity.

Right there on that edge, right underneath the Golden Gate Bridge, these two huge, energetic, powerful bodies of water come together. As a result of this edge, the San Francisco Bay contains incredible richness of biodiversity, making it one of California's most important natural habitats. It's a place where there's magic. It's a sweet spot.

Apple's Guy Kawasaki said, "What really matters happens at the edges." I know I already mentioned this quote, but it bears repeating. If ever there was one quote that summed up my whole outlook on life and work and the creative process, this would be it. It's all about the edges.

My brain goes straight to optimization when I start to think about edges. Optimization is a mathematical term with a very specific definition. In everyday life, we bandy about the words *optimal* or *optimize*, but the vast majority of us use it casually without understanding what it means. Usually, when we use these words, we mean that something is really, really good. It's so good that we probably can't think of something we might change about it. That's the colloquial meaning of *optimal*.

But in math, *optimum* is a very real, specific, and calculable value. To find the optimum mathematically, you first define the objective— the thing you're trying to optimize—and then you set constraints. These constraints come from various sources. They may be set by the laws of physics. They could be set by monetary or time limitations. They can be set by personal preferences. They can be set by any number of real or imagined boundaries that you're putting around the problem that you have to solve.

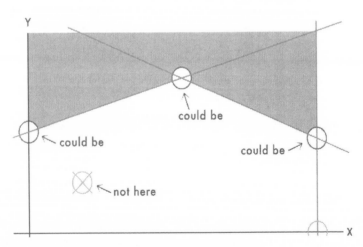

Optimization at the Edges

When you go to find the optimal solution, the optimal point is never located out in the nebulous middle of the solution space. It's always slammed right up against the edges of two or more constraints. The optimal solutions usually sit in the corners right on the edges. Those, in essence, are the sweet spots.

So, I invite you to step back from any negative connotation that the word *edge* might have for you. It might sound scary, like a precipice or a cliff face that you might fall over if you get too close. Instead, I encourage you to think of an edge as the place where magic happens. It happens at the intersection of two boundaries, of two opposing forces. That's where we start to see the integration of two opposites. That's the sweet spot.

We've also talked about how we might have negative connotations around the word *boundaries*. Sometimes it can feel as if boundaries highlight what we can't do, so they seem limiting. But what if we saw boundaries, limitations, or constraints as the genesis of the sweet spot? The sweet spot wouldn't exist without edges to run up against.

This doesn't mean that we should neglect thinking about our constraints. It doesn't mean that we shouldn't question everything to make sure that we're not putting false boundaries or limiting beliefs up in front of us that may be holding us back instead of creating opportunities. But we can take the healthy structure that's formed by the boundaries and constraints to get to the sweet spot.

At the edges, we start to see the magic that happens while flowing around the spiral. We start to see the edge between Inspiration and Implementation. We can see the edge between Implementation and Investigation. We see the edge between Investigation and Introspection and the edge between Introspection and Inspiration. Each edge is where growth happens. The edge is where forward momentum is generated. In the spiral, we are constantly dancing across the edges.

It's at the edges where we see the dichotomies start to break down as opposites come together. At the beginning of this book, we talked about the Balance Myth—how a static state of balance isn't realistic or healthy. I suggest to you now that integration is the alternative. Instead of balance, look for integration: the integration of structure and flow, the integration of masculine and feminine, the integration of action and rest, the integration of introversion and extraversion, the integration of any two concepts that seem to oppose each other.

These integrations are edges. The edge is the place where you're still able to see that there are two separate conditions, but they start to blend and intertwine. When things start to blend and intertwine, you really have a dance. You have a potent cocktail that's powerful enough to birth new creative endeavors into the world.

I'm challenging you. The next time you go looking for balance, even if it feels like something that's healthy, could you look for integration instead? Could you look at the edge and appreciate the coming together of two seemingly disjointed, separate, and even opposite things? Could you appreciate the gifts that each phase brings? Could you examine that edge more closely and look for the magic? Because that edge, that boundary, that place of integration is where it happens.

There's no true wall there. There's no true wall between the ocean and the bay. There's no true wall between the masculine and the feminine, or the introvert and the extravert, or the structure and the flow.

There's no wall.

There's nothing that prevents us from crossing over. That's part of the magic. In each of these dichotomies, we remain separate but also joined. The resulting diversity of thought, capability, and opportunity is the manifestation of the magic at the edges.

CHAPTER TWENTY-ONE

Intuition

WE HUMANS FOOL OURSELVES INTO THINKING that there are step-by-step processes that will solve all of our problems. "If I just follow this diet, I'll get to my ideal weight." "If I just buy this curriculum, I'll be fluent in a foreign language."

There's no guarantee that any system will work for you. The human mind likes to attach to a system as if the system is the answer. But as you've seen, a system is just a tool. The answer is inside you.

I didn't write this book to tell you that if you meet four out of five sets of criteria, you're ready to move to the next phase of the spiral. Or if you meet four out of five sets of these other criteria, you need to reevaluate your vision because it's not serving your needs anymore.

Your own personal mystery is part of the process. It may feel frustrating, but that's really the beauty of it. The beauty is that you get to know yourself. You raise your self-awareness, and you're the better for it. This is why entrepreneurship has been called the best personal development program you'll ever embark on. You have to know yourself.

The spiral isn't prescriptive. This process is intuitive and adaptable to you as an individual with all your quirks and uniqueness.

The spiral is a framework to help you understand yourself better. It's an observation about the human condition and life on Earth. You get to choose if it's consistent with your experience and if you want to use it to help you come to know yourself better. Knowing yourself better is the key to doing your work in the world, living your best life, and feeling great about what you are creating for yourself and for others.

The answers to all of the questions you ask yourself in the dark—"Is it enough?" or "When do I move on?"—exist in your self-awareness. Do you truly know yourself? Can you hear the voice of your intuition, listen to it, and trust it? Learning the spiral is a form of self-awareness and listening to your intuition. You are a human and a citizen of Earth. Therefore, you work in cycles. When you need to tune into that intuition, you don't find yourself saying, "My God, all of my emotional indicators are pegged at fear and anger! I don't know what to do!" Because you know the spiral framework, you have a context for figuring out where you just came from and where you might be heading next. This knowing can help you consciously select the tools from your toolbox that can help.

As I write this, I just went through a long phase (six months or so) of shedding structure and living completely in flow. This is weird for me because my "dominant hand" is structure. But I felt stifled and caged at the time, so I let go of many things that looked like structure. I shed schedules and commitments. I stopped setting goals. I refused to start any new programs or routines. I took structure down to the bare minimum. And I felt as if I could breathe for the first time in a long while. I was able to figure myself out in my new role as CEO of a tech company and to overhaul my vision (yet again) in the midst of the chaos of parenting young children.

But recently, I've felt a little scattered. I've felt ungrounded. I've felt as if I lost my place in the sheet music of my life, and that's made me frustrated and sad. And because I know myself, including my dominant mode of operation, which is structure, I realize that the unsettled drifting I've been experiencing means that it's time to inhale again. It's time to reintroduce structure. Gently, compassionately, and slowly, it's time to establish routines, patterns, and commitments. So, I've joined a tae kwon do class. I've started back up with my therapist. The new structure feels good. I'm back in the groove.

I'm not fooling myself that this structure will serve me forever. I'm not fooling myself that there's some perfect level of structure that I can achieve and that if I maintain it, I'll never have to adjust again. No, I'm a cyclical being. So, though structure is my dominant way of being, I'm sure there will come a time again in six months or twelve when I feel caged and stifled once again. And then I will exhale, shed, release into flow, and give myself the gift of meeting my own needs in that present moment.

The spiral provides you with the self-awareness you need to self-diagnose or figure out what you need in any given moment. You'll never say, "Crap, I missed step four in a twelve-step process, and now I'm hosed!" Or, "Now I have to start over!" (You don't have to start over, for crying out loud, unless it serves your highest good.)

CHAPTER TWENTY-TWO

True Dichotomy

WE SPENT THE BEGINNING OF THIS BOOK SMASHING the idea that these concepts are opposed and separate. In some cases, they're gradations on a spectrum. In some cases, they're qualities that can work together. They're all part of the same spiral. Even if they sit on opposite sides of a spiral, the flow of the universe—the flow of our very existence—fluctuates back and forth between one side of a dichotomy and the other. One side is not "good" while the other is "evil." It's only our human minds that place labels like that.

But as we progress through these cycles of structure and flow, there's a real tension and, perhaps, a true dichotomy that we need to deal with and hold space for. There's tension between holding a vision for a future that we have not yet created and being present in this moment.

This is a dichotomy that really does exist. How can we have the impetus, the desire, and the motivation to create something new if we are truly content and joyful in the present moment and fully immersed in what's happening right now?

Similarly, if we are truly content with ourselves and with the state of things in the present moment, why would we then seek out an opportunity to change the future?

There is space for both sides of this dichotomy. It's really the core of the spiral.

On one side of the spiral, the core is being able to flow and to rest and to pause. The gift of the spiral is contentment in this moment, because we're able to find bliss and joy in the here and now—the phase we're in. In doing so, we open ourselves to inspiration.

But it's also through the creative spiral that we know that it's also possible to put our nose to the grindstone, do the work, and take the action that needs to be taken to realize a vision.

Not only are these two states possible and part of the spiral, but each is necessary to move the other forward. In order to reach these states of blissful contentment in the present moment, we take action to improve ourselves. That external, action-taking, masculine sentiment is how our culture operates. We are constantly working to ensure we have these states of bliss. Then, all too often, we ignore the bliss when it comes, and we say, "It's not good enough yet. I don't have it yet."

It's important to look at the flip side. The inspiration never comes unless you're present in the moment. True innovation never comes unless you allow yourself to be still, be here, be right now, be empty.

It's like respiration. You breathe in, and you breathe out. You breathe in, and you breathe out. No one questions that in order to breathe in, you have to create space by breathing out first. No one questions that in order to breathe out, there has to be air in your lungs, which means you must have breathed in. These things happen naturally, automatically, without having to think about them.

The fluctuation between structure and flow is as easy and as natural as breathing in and out. Breathing is actually all about the present moment. While you breathe in, you never think, "Oh my gosh, what happens when I need to breathe out? Am I going to be ready for it? What if I'm not? Maybe I should do something right now to prepare for breathing out." That never happens. You simply breathe in and trust that when it's time to breathe out, you'll be able to do it.

To me, that's what presence in the moment means. It's being okay with whatever part of the spiral you're in and understanding that it's good, healthy, and just what you need. You don't worry about whether the spiral will come around again or not. This is easier said than done, of course. I myself am terrible at remembering exactly where I am in the spiral. I get frustrated. I wish I was in another spiral phase. I feel as if I should be preparing for the time when the spiral comes around again instead of just understanding that where I am is where I am and it's healthy and good.

We humans, with our higher executive function, are able to apply the breathing to something useful. We're able to take our breathing and direct it, to slow our bodies down and ground ourselves in meditation, or to focus on the effort required to give birth to a child, or to fuel our bodies with the appropriate oxygen for intense exercise. We take the simple, involuntary act of breathing, and we apply it to something bigger than the act itself.

Without breath, there is no meditation. Without breath, there is no childbirth. Without breath, there is no exercise and no athletic achievement. Therein lies the key to holding space for your presence in the moment; your contentment in the moment, along with your vision of something better. Can you apply your bliss and joy and contentment and "enoughness" in the moment? Can you apply them to the future? Can you apply them to moving your vision into something better?

It's a dichotomy, yes. But like all dichotomies that we've talked about, they don't sit on opposite sides of a spectrum. They work together in integration to create your best life.

You are enough. Right now. Just as you are. This needs to be said over and over and over because we obsess about being better, being stronger and faster, and creating the next big thing.

I know you will be faster and stronger, and you will be innovative, and you will create the next big thing. You will fulfill all of those things you're meant to fulfill, and you will evolve.

You will because you *can* and because you *are*. I believe in you, and I think you know it's true too. All of this is possible in the future. But I think it's harder to believe and harder to remember that you are enough in this moment—that you already have everything you need in the here and now. Even as you move on to acquire new skills and new experiences to help you move forward into the future, right now, right where you are, you have what you need.

You can come back and read this section again when you forget or feel frustrated.

These present moments are the building blocks of the future you're creating. That's how you hold space for both the vision and the present. Don't lose sight of the moment you're in, blinded by pursuit of the vision.

When I was growing up, I never thought about the present moment. I was obsessed with the future. I did get to do a lot of fun things. I did make good choices and have enjoyable times. But I never stopped to appreciate how important each individual moment was. I never stopped to notice that in each moment, I was already enough.

Allow yourself to be where you are, and have faith that you'll come around the other side of the spiral. When you do, you'll be able to use those gifts at that time, in that place. Then, you can direct these natural cycles just as you can direct your inhales and your exhales to build something bigger and more important. Using the building blocks of the now to create tomorrow, you can build the vision to create your life and your work, to create the change that you want to see in the world.

CHAPTER TWENTY-THREE

A Glimpse of the Future

IT'S EASY TO TALK ABOUT EMBRACING NATURAL CYCLES when it's about you operating as an individual. One podcast host who heard me speak on the topics of integration and embracing the spiral told me, "I can feel my energy settle, like it's coming right back into my being. Instead of feeling scattered, I feel grounded." It's incredibly powerful to feel that shift.

But how do we bring this perspective, this awareness, into our interactions with the rest of the world? How do we bring it into a world and a culture steeped in toxic masculinity? How do we bring it into a world that's having labor pains birthing a newer, higher level of existence?

When my primary business and mission was to coach individuals who wanted to start their own businesses, keeping this perspective was relatively easy. I say relatively because I first had to make that perspective shift. Then, when I was down in the thick of the work, it was tough to always have a bearing on where I was in the spiral. But generally speaking, once I ask myself, "Where are you in the spiral?" it's pretty easy for me to home in on my location and reconnect to the cycle.

When we bring these skills out into the world, outside of our own sphere of control, the waters get murky. How do your spirals interact with those of your family, your colleagues, your clients, and—holy crap—the multitude of people you're around every day? And then add the complication that you're interacting with people at varying levels of awareness. The spiral is there whether you acknowledge it or not. But there's a wide range of awareness of this need for masculine/feminine integration, ranging from totally open to unaware to completely opposed to any discussion of the subject. And when you walk into a boardroom or classroom or any kind of community gathering place, you can't be entirely sure what kind of mix you've got there.

So, what are we to do?

This is part of the revolution, friend. This is how we raise planetary consciousness in a practical way. We get out of our bubble. We find the courage to lead with empathy, compassion, and an attitude of service. We are willing to experiment and play with cyclical and integrative concepts, and we lead others to play along with us. We must do this. This is our sacred responsibility.

If you have awakened, this is the mission to which you are called.

Individuals will lead the way.

In order to have integrative communities and organizations, we need to start with integrative-thinking individuals who embrace a spiral, cyclical process as normal, healthy, and desirable. So just being present with this knowing is the first step.

But it's not enough to stop there. Knowing and leveraging the spiral process for yourself isn't your only responsibility. You have to have the courage to bring it with you into the old cultural structures. You have to have the courage to be the beacon, the way-shower, the path-lighter.

And it does take courage. As a coach, I've worked with many other lightworkers—coaches, spiritual healers, and others. It feels safe to talk about these principles with those people, because we have a common willingness to explore the larger threads that tie us all together. My coaching work was the fertile ground in which these ideas took shape. They were rooted in design principles I brought from spacecraft engineering. But at the time I learned those principles as an engineer, I hadn't yet awoken. Becoming a coach was part of my awakening into the awareness of up-leveling consciousness.

By the time I went back to work in technology—the renewable energy industry—I'd awoken. I had an arsenal of new skills beyond project management and system performance analysis. I came back to technology with intuition, empathy, a desire to be of service, extreme authenticity, a working knowledge of my own personal power, and a sense of how my cycles worked. But going into boardrooms or sales calls, I felt myself start to slip into old patterns. There was no place for spirituality and intuition in this "real" world. This was serious business.

But of course, any place that leaves out spirituality, intuition, and empathy is *not* the real world after all. The actual real world is rife with that stuff, and without them, what kind of strange, robotic world would we have?

I learned this in one of my early sales calls. We were on a conference call with a potential client who'd been listening to a sales pitch from a very large, old-school, intensely masculine company trying to sell him a piece of equipment. The company reps had basically steamrolled the client with how big and important they were, how much experience they had, and why he should start now, now, now!

When we got on the phone with this client later that day, I started by making sure I truly understood his vision for the project. We went deep into his subject-matter knowledge. Then, I described how my company could be of service and help him wade through the mire of options in front of him. The relief in his voice was palpable as he exclaimed, "You are exactly what I need! Can you help me?" It wasn't about selling him a product, which was the old way of doing things. It was about truly understanding him as a person and as a visionary, and then offering to support his vision. Offering to support someone else's vision takes a heck of a lot of intuition and empathy. And a lot of courage and hard work too. That's how real-world work gets done. That's how we change the world.

So, I'm calling on you now. You have the tools you need to birth your true work into the world. You have the tools you need to support the life and work that you want to build. And you also have the tools you need to embark on the work of infiltrating the old structures and transforming them into something healthier, more aware, more vibrant, more integrative, and more whole.

It doesn't take a rocket scientist to do this.

All it takes is for you to have the courage to embrace your own spiral.

Acknowledgements

You won't be shocked to learn that developing this book and the ideas it holds was both an iterative and an integrative process. I have seen all the threads of almost everything I've ever learned in engineering, in business, in spirituality, in life logistics, and in personal development come together to weave this masterpiece of an idea. Since this work has pulled from every area of my life and self-awareness, nearly everyone who has been part of my journey has served to pull on these threads or to hold up a mirror so that I can see more clearly.

In particular, I want to extend my thanks to a specific set of allies, who have been there with me on the journey.

My book coach, editor, and publisher, Amy Collette—where do I begin? Almost from the moment the words "I'm going to write the book" fell from my lips, Amy appeared from the ether. She's been everything I didn't know I needed: cheerleader, advisor, grief counselor, therapist, co-conspirator, and fellow nerd. From the study room at the Golden Library, the table strewn with sticky notes, where our voices rose and jaws dropped to the moment the eagle swooped overhead the first time we said the subtitle, there's been magic the whole way. There's no way this book would be half what it is without her support and hard work. That we share our name— the beloveds—seems like no accident. And a tip of the hat to the divine Carol Wolff who had the wisdom and good grace to introduce us.

Also on the publishing team here, I would be remiss if I didn't gush over the work of Melody Christian for both the incredible cover and interior graphic design. She brilliantly made the spiral come to life, crawling inside my brain when I hadn't the words. She also sat through several lessons in mathematics and physics with the long-suffering patience of a saint. And thanks to Lauren Brombert, whose thoroughness and consistency made my words readable.

My mentor, business coach, master (to my apprentice), and friend, Farnoosh Brock was the first person to tell me I could design my own work in the world. And not only did she tell me—she lived it herself, showing me that *engineer* is just a title, just a facet of the diamond, not the whole of our existence. I've known her for years at this point (crazy, but true) and she still always knows exactly what to say, whether it's praise or tough love. She wrote this incredibly beautiful and complimentary foreword, which is more than I could have asked.

Back in 2015, Farnoosh assembled a mastermind of women with big ideas, and we embarked on a Year of Transformation together. I have to thank my mastermind sisters, Rachael Tiow, Yelena Kaganovsky, and Aki Raymer for holding the space I needed to detach from job-title-as-identity and integrate all the disparate parts of myself into a cohesive person. I especially thank my mastermind sister Tamara DaSantos for diving into the depths of this book with me and helping the book be all it can be. And a special shout out to Tamara's brother-in-law, John Schofield, for the word "catalyst," an integral part of the subtitle.

I'm eternally grateful to the first cohort of the Spiral Business Development Mastermind, who unwittingly helped me solidify the power behind this framework. Rosanne Sliuzas, Lori Bertazzon, and Vidya Ananthanarayanan have always been cheerleaders, light-bringers, and way-showers on this journey. Lois English and Sabra Kay have walked with me from the earliest days of the spiral right into the very first readings of this book, and it wouldn't be what it is without you both.

Thanks to Maggie Sullivan, Kelly Bezjak, and Christy Edwards for having the courage to be fellow engineer-poets.

Tonia Sturdy is one of my high school best friends, who has always loved me in full and known so much of the depths of me. She helped me in the stuck places when I couldn't see the forest and helped me navigate the trees. Time and distance mean nothing, as it turns out. She still gets me, through and through.

My heart, my sister, my bosom friend, Kelly Parnigoni—words fail me. We've been together through the hardest parts of the spiral and through the glorious discovery of ourselves in the midst of the muck. I'll be your wingman anytime.

And finally to Travis Simpkins—cheerleader, confidante, teammate, lover. Thanks for honesty, for hugs from behind, for validation, for taking the kids, and for a lifetime of adventure—sometimes more adventure than is strictly necessary.

Resources

Some of the following resources are mentioned in the book, and some influenced the ideas behind it. All of them are near and dear to my heart.

Burnett, Bill, and Dave Evans. *Designing Your Life: How to Build a Well-Lived, Joyful Life.* Alfred A. Knopf, 2018.

Cameron, Julia. *The Artist's Way: a Spiritual Path to Higher Creativity.* TarcherPerigee, 1992.

Campbell, Joseph. *The Hero with a Thousand Faces.* New World Library, 2008.

Christensen, Clayton M. *The Innovator's Dilemma: When New Technologies Cause Great Firms to Fail.* Harvard Business Review Press, 2016

Godin, Seth. *Icarus Deception: How High Will You Fly?* Portfolio, 2014.

Godin, Seth. *Linchpin: Are You Indispensable?* Piatkus, 2018.

Johnson, Crockett. *Harold and the Purple Crayon.* HarperFestival, an Imprint of HarperCollins, 2016.

Kawasaki, Guy, and Michele Moreno. *Rules for Revolutionaries: the Capitalist Manifesto for Creating and Marketing New Products and Services.* HarperCollins World, 2000.

Kelley, Tom, and David Kelley. *Creative Confidence: Unleashing the Creative Potential within Us All.* William Collins, 2015.

LaPorte, Danielle. *The Desire Map: a Guide to Creating Goals with Soul.* Sounds True, 2014.

Martin, Roger. *The Design of Business: Why Design Thinking Is the next Competitive Advantage.* Harvard Business Press, 2009.

Pollio, Vitruvius, et al. *The Ten Books on Architecture.* Architecture Classics, 2017.

Pressfield, Steven. *The War of Art: Break through the Blocks and Win Your Inner Creative Battles.* Black Irish Entertainment, 2012.

Raworth, Kate. *Doughnut Economics: Seven Ways to Think like a 21st-Century Economist.* Chelsea Green, 2018.

Schulz, Mona Lisa. *The New Feminine Brain: Developing Your Intuitive Genius.* Free Press, 2006.

Design thinking courses: https://www.ideou.com/

Headspace App for meditation:
https://www.headspace.com/

Insight Timer App for meditation:
https://insighttimer.com/

Architect Your Business course
http://amysimpkins.com/aybcourse

Solar system vortex video:
https://youtu.be/0jHsq36_NTU

Pendulum video: https://www.khanacademy.org/science/ap-physics-1/simple-harmonic-motion-ap/simple-pendulums-ap/v/pendulum

About the Author

Amy Simpkins has an engineer's brain and a poet's heart. Her life's work has been centered around the integration of seemingly unrelated things and the subsequent solution of wickedly hard problems.

Ms. Simpkins is a holistic entrepreneurship coach and a vision architect for professionals and business owners. She helps people with big ideas weave all of the complex magic within themselves together, so they show up with access to all of their innate superpowers and make their impossible dreams possible and profitable. She has been helping innovators implement their ideas since 2013.

Ms. Simpkins is also CEO of the renewable energy startup muGrid Analytics. muGrid solves problems at the edge of energy technology and economics using math and modeling, and is dedicated to creating a sustainable energy future for the planet, one project at a time.

As a young, female executive in the tech world, she puts her theories about disruptive innovation and bringing your whole self to work into practice every single day.

Previously, Ms. Simpkins designed, integrated, and operated spacecraft at Lockheed Martin Space Systems Company. During her 10-year tenure as an aspiring Spacecraft Systems Architect, she worked on diverse programs such as Juno, Stardust-NExT, Orion, and Space Radar, as well as spent time in dynamic idea incubation groups for new and exciting innovation.

Ms. Simpkins holds an SB in Aeronautics and Astronautics from the Massachusetts Institute of Technology and an MS in Astronautical Engineering from the University of Southern California.

She is a messy chef, a world traveler, a taekwondo orange belt, a homeschooling mom of three, and a tough cookie in the Colorado backcountry.

Contact the author at amysimpkins.com